THE AUSTRALIAN
Women's Weekly
#Veganlife

#Veganlife

ORIGINAL

CONTENTS

Plant-based LIVING

A vegan diet is wholly plant-based and excludes all animal products. In addition to the obvious – no meat, seafood, eggs and dairy products, honey and gelatine are also off limits on this diet. There are also some surprising places that animal products can lurk, to find out more on what they are, see our list on page 11.

It wasn't all that long ago that a vegan diet was considered an extreme lifestyle choice, raising questions, like 'what is left to eat?' and 'won't I miss out on important nutrients?' Fast forward to today and the chances are if you are not already a full-time vegan yourself, that you know someone who is, either vegetarian or vegan, or dabbles in either diet. After all, there are many reasons people choose to embrace the diet, from concern for animal welfare, to environmental and health reasons. Worldwide, eating a vegetarian diet is on the increase, while in Australia 2.1 million (11.2 percent) of Australians are eating this way. Making the leap from vegetarianism to veganism (or directly to veganism) is not so hard when you know that the array of foods that will fuel your diet is expansive, incorporating common ingredients, and best yet – it doesn't mean forgoing great-tasting food.

While, there is evidence that eating a predominantly plant-based diet is a healthy one it is not suitable for children. Those on a vegan diet tend to weigh less than their meat-eating counterparts and are at a lower risk of developing type-2 diabetes, heart disease, and some cancers. This is because a well-balanced plant-based diet includes a wide array of plant matter, fibre and tends to be low fat. As with any diet it is possible to misstep and make poor choices and eat too much fat or sugar. With a vegan diet care must be undertaken to ensure sufficient intake of vitamin B12, calcium, iodine, iron, zinc, and omega-3 fatty acids. When you know which plant foods include these essential nutrients you are able to achieve a balanced diet.

To help you on your path to a tasty vegan life, the chapters in this book have been designed to match an array of lifestyle scenarios. Wake Up; start the day ditching eggs, for a delicious tofu scramble. For active types, head straight to the Active Life chapter, for snacks on the go, desk-draw treats and protein-fuelled smoothies. For transport-friendly lunches flick to the Out and About chapter. Mid-week dinners present a time challenge to any cook, so depending on your mood or wallet; choose from the Lazy Vegan or Cheap Vegan chapters to find meal solutions. When the weather warms, explore the lighter offering in Go Raw or Summer Vegan chapters; when it cools, find solace with nourishing soups and stews in Comfort Food. Fun fast food options haven't been forgotten either, whether it is food to chill out with while TV binging or a yearning for fish and chips. There are clever twists on these and other favourites in our Fast Food chapter. Entertaining with non-vegan friends might sound like the ultimate conundrum; is it truly possibly, you wonder to impress with vegan food? Undoubtedly! Just take a peek at the stellar offerings in Weekends, here we prove that vegan food can really be everyone's life.

THERE ARE MANY REASONS PEOPLE CHOOSE TO EMBRACE A VEGAN DIET, FROM CONCERN FOR ANIMAL WELFARE, TO ENVIRONMENTAL AND HEALTH REASONS.

ESSENTIAL NUTRIENTS

A well-balanced vegan diet should include a wide range of colourful vegetables and fruits. With so much choice on offer be guided by nature and use the seasons as your inspiration for the best selection. For the building blocks of a good diet, eat widely to ensure that you are capturing your nutrient needs from the following essential nutrients.

Proteins Allow our bodies to build new proteins and are fundamental to all the processes our bodies undertake, from building cell and muscle tissue to the health of our hair, skin and nails. And unlike carbs, protein is not stored in our bodies, so a good daily supply is essential. Animal proteins are considered complete as they contain all essential amino acids, while most plant based proteins need to be combined to be complete. Animal proteins can also bring with them unhealthy saturated fats. Luckily for the vegan, protein needs are easily met with legumes (dried and canned lentils, chickpeas, cannellini beans, kidney beans, borlotti beans, black-eye beans and green and yellow split peas), nuts (almonds, cashews, peanuts, pecans, pistachios, macadamias and walnuts), seeds (pepitas, sunflower seeds, linseeds, chia seeds, sesame seeds and tahini), soy products (tofu, tempeh, soy milk and miso), grains and grain substitutes/pseudo-grains (amaranth, barley, buckwheat, freekeh, oats, rice faro, millet, polenta, quinoa and wheat-based products like burghul).

Carbs While there is a trend towards low carb diets, not all carbs are created equal. Plant-based foods, certain starch vegetables and legumes are often quite high in carbs, however they are also high in dietary fibre. It is important to differentiate between these valuable unrefined carbohydrate sources and refined sources from sugar, fizzy drinks, baked goods and other similarly nutritionally empty foods.

Calcium Vegans need to include plenty of dark green leafy vegetables (silver beet, asian greens, kale, watercress etc), soy products (tofu and soy milk), sesame seeds, legumes (black beans, soy beans, chickpeas, cannellini beans and borlotti beans) and calcium-enriched cereals.

Iodine is needed for healthy thyroid function which in turn aids metabolism. For vegans who omit seafood from thier diet, meeting this need can be a challenge, especially since certain vegetables contain a compound that can thwart absorption. Sea vegetables such as nori (think sushi wrappers), wakame or kombu are good sources, or use a little iodised salt to meet your requirements. Check with your doctor before taking supplements if you have a thyroid issue.

Omega-3 fatty acids Provide all manner of health benefits, from reducing the risk of heart disease, to reducing cognitive decline. For meat eaters they are readily available from fish and eggs; however there are also plenty of plant-based alternatives, such as grains, legumes, nuts (especially walnuts) and flaxseeds in which they are found.

Vitamin B12 As this nutrient is only found in meat, incorporate foods fortified with vitamin B12, such as some cereals, plant-based milks and soy products. A supplement can be taken for healthy blood cells and the prevention of anaemia.

Zinc Is another nutrient that, like iron, isn't absorbed quite as well from plant sources as it is from meat. Vegans should include whole grains, nuts, pepitas (pumpkin seed kernels), soy products (tempeh and tofu) and wheatgerm in their diet.

GETTING ENOUGH IRON

Sourcing sufficient iron on a plant-based diet is often top of mind for many people. Iron is an essential nutrient as it carries oxygen to the blood. Iron deficiency (anaemia) is not more marked in those on a plant-based diet than meat eaters, though iron stores are shown to be lower in studies of vegans. In the general population deficiencies are more common among menstruating women, female athletes and children.

Iron is found in food in two forms: heme and non-heme iron. Meat comprises of 40 percent heme iron and 60 percent non-heme iron, while all iron in plant-based food is heme. Since plant sources are not as bioavailable, vegans should be especially aware of the foods that are high in iron and techniques to increase absorption, such as combining with vitamin C rich foods (see below), which are consumed with abundance anyway on a vegan diet. Doing so can elicit a six-fold increase in the uptake of iron. Recommendations for iron intake for vegans are generally advised as being as much as double that of meat eaters.

Luckily for vegans there are also plants that are both iron and vitamin C rich, and in these the iron is readily absorbed. There are also foods to be aware of that can hamper absorption, such as calcium supplements and the tannins found in tea and coffee. To avoid interference from these, consume them separately from main meals.

While meat is often thought as superior for iron needs, on a calorie basis plant foods can provide a superior return. For example, 100 calories of spinach (2¼ cups cooked), while a lot spinach to eat, provides 15.5mg iron. In contrast the same calories of a steak yields 0.9mg iron. To achieve the same iron intake from steak 1700 calories must be consumed.

Iron rich foods: soy beans, blackstrap molasses, lentils, tofu, chickpeas, tempeh, black-eyed beans, silver beet, kidney beans, black beans, potato, prunes, quinoa, tahini, peas, cashews, bok choy, dried figs and apricots, almonds, spinach broccoli, sunflower seeds and peptitas.

Vitamin C rich foods: capsicum (bell peppers), citrus, strawberries, tomatoes, kale, cauliflower and sweet potatoes.

MEAL PREP LIKE A BOSS

A degree of planning with shopping and prepping will assist in keeping you from entering a food rut. Ensure the kitchen is always well stocked; dedicate one day a week to preparing a weekly menu and shopping list. This way you are not pressed to think of what to cook after a busy tiring day. Sunday is often a good day for full-time workers to jump into the kitchen and make a head start on the upcoming week's cooking. If Sundays are taken, instead aim to meal prep on Monday or mid-week.

PLANNING AND MEAL PREP ARE GREAT STEPS TOWARDS HEALTHY AND STRESS-FREE EATING, AS THERE'S NO DECISION MAKING REQUIRED AT MEAL TIMES, YOU JUST NEED TO SIT DOWN AND EAT.

Bulk shop dry goods weekly Save time by doing a regular bulk shop of all your dry ingredients, as well as longer lasting vegetables, so all you need to shop for are perishables.

Organise the pantry A clean organised pantry helps you find items quickly. Transfer opened items to clear labelled and dated glass storage containers. Aim to always have a selection of staples, such as canned beans, tomatoes and grains.

Slice, dice and chop ahead Certain vegetables lend themselves to advance chopping – carrots, cabbage, broccoli, cauliflower, capsicum, pumpkin and sweet potato. Keep each vegetable separate. Avoid prepping soft and moist vegetables (onion and garlic) and herbs as they will oxidise.

Cook double Look for recipes that can be doubled and eaten over multiple nights. Not all food will last all week in the fridge so aim to also use the freezer for storage.

Find ingredient overlaps When you are creating your weekly menu look for recipes that share ingredients like rice, quinoa or leafy greens so that you can cook them ahead.

Containers Purchase good quality BPA-free plastic or glass containers for food storage. Use plastic for the freezer as glass containers can expand and crack. And don't forget labels.

Equipment Take advantage of a mandoline, V-slicer, food processor or Thermomix, if you have one, to assist with the prep.

DECODING LABELS

In order to make an informed choice around the consumption of animal-based products it is necessary to know the names of certain animal-based ingredients that can be hidden away in everyday food stuffs. The good thing to know is the more you eat minimally processed foods, the less likely you are to encounter them.

Hidden dairy Vegans avoid dairy and therefore animal rennet, a coagulate commonly used in cheese making. Other dairy-based ingredients to watch out for are: casein, whey, lactalbumin, lactose, lactulose, nougat candy and ghee (derived from butter) and the Indian dairy-based cheese paneer. Lactic acid is used in beer, sauerkraut, pickles and products that use bacterial fermentation.

Hidden seafood products Anchovies are hidden away in caesar dressings and many brands of worcestershire sauce, while fish sauce is a common ingredient in Thai curries pastes and takeaways. Isinglass a fish-based gelatine-like product can turn up in alcoholic drinks and jelly desserts.

Hidden meat products Gelatine is in marshmallows, gummy-style confectionery and is a common coating for pills. Sugar can be refined through bone char, though this is not the case with Australian produced sugar. Tallow, animal shortening, pops up in refried beans, tortillas and ready-made pastries.

Hidden egg products Egg yolk is common in dried ribbon pasta. Albumin, derived from egg whites may be used as a fining agent and may not be declared on wines and liqueurs labels. Check websites for vegan-friendly brands.

HELPFUL LINKS

Animals Australia
www.animalsaustralia.org
Australia's leading animal protection organisation, spearheading important investigations and campaigns.

Choose Cruelty Free (CCF)
www.choosecrueltyfree.org.au
This independent, not-for profit organisation produces The Choose Cruelty Free List, a booklet listing companies and brand names that operate under a cruelty-free ethic to help consumers make informed choices.

People for the Ethical Treatment of Animals (PETA) www.peta.org.au
The largest global organisation in the world for animal protection, whose mission statement is – 'animals are not ours to eat, wear, experiment on, use for entertainment, or abuse in any other way.' The local website includes useful links to food, fashion and vegan beauty retailers, as well as campaigns.

The Cruelty Free Shop
www.crueltyfreeshop.com.au
With retail stores in three Australian states, plus an online shop of over 1,500 vegan items.

Vegan Australia www.veganaustralia.org.au
This website provides a wide range of services to new and existing vegans from event listings, news, vegan nutrition to details on campaigns.

Barnivore www.barnivore.com
An online vegan alcohol directory.

WHILE AT FIRST IT MAY SEEM THAT AVOIDING ANIMAL PRODUCTS IS FRAUGHT, THERE ARE MANY WEBSITES TO HELP YOU AND ENCOURAGINGLY, SAVVY FOOD COMPANIES RECOGNISE THAT A VEGAN-LIFESTYLE IS AN IMPORTANT PART OF THEIR MARKET SHARE AND ARE ASSISTING WITH LABELLING THEIR PRODUCTS.

The right balance

YOUR DAY ON A PLATE

Active person

It is important if you fall into this category, especially if you are female and pre-menopausal, to ensure that you avoid restrictive food eating patterns, or you risk an inadequate dietary intake and optimum health. For the active vegan, incorporate energy dense foods such as nuts, tofu, tempeh and other quality protein at every meal. Since vegetable proteins don't include all the necessary amino acids required, it is necessary to combine a variety of proteins throughout the day to meet the requirements, for example, combine legumes and grains or legumes and seeds. Since plant-based proteins are not as easily digested as meat derived ones, it is advised that vegans consume 10 percent more. If you are vegan and super active it is especially important to target iron-rich foods and monitor your iron stores. To ensure sufficient calcium intake look for calcium-rich vegan food, such as almonds, leafy greens and broccoli. If you drink soy or nut milks look for those that are fortified with 100mg per 100ml milk. Never skip breakfast, always start with a breakfast that balances carbs and proteins. Lunch is equally important and can be tricky to plan for if you are on the go. Sandwiches with nut spreads and that include fillings like hummus are handy, or pick quinoa-based salads, and in cooler months, soups with legumes in a thermos or tofu or legume-based burgers in a bun. You may need to top up during the day on energy dense snacks, for ideas on these look at our Active Vegan chapter. A vegan dinner should include a wide array of colourful vegetable, proteins and carbs.

Moderately active person

The nutritional requirements of a moderately active person are very similar to that of an active person. The main difference between the two is that your overall kilojoule requirements will be less. Also, your carb requirements may be reduced. As with a vegan diet in general, balance and eating widely from all the different sectors of plant-based foods are the key things to ensure that you are capturing vital nutrients and are not missing out on certain key nutritional requirements that can be harder to meet on a vegan diet (see Essential Nutrients on pages 8 & 9). There are many foods that are vegan, however this does not mean that they are necessarily healthy, in fact many manufactured vegan substitutes, burgers, not-dogs and ready-made meals are the fast food equivalents of meat-based ones and can be laden with not so useful bulking agents that can add unnecessarily to your kilojoule quota.

ACROSS EACH DAY LOOK TO FILL YOUR PLATE WITH A WIDE ARRAY OF COLOURFUL VEGETABLES, FRUITS, WHOLEGRAINS, LEGUMES, NUTS AND SEEDS, AS WELL INCLUDE HEALTHY FATS, LIKE AVOCADO AND EXTRA VIRGIN OLIVE OIL FOR A BALANCED DIET.

Also, just because sweet treats are vegan doesn't afford them health-food status. While it is fun as a vegan to be able to indulge in the odd doughnut, brownie and other sweet treats, just as with mainstream treats, they should be kept occasional.

Fridge basics

Your fridge in particular will look a little different on a vegan diet. Butter, cheese and other dairy items will all require a re-think, so too do stocks, mayo and pastry. Thankfully there are lots of delicious vegan options, and better yet they can all be made at home (see pages 16 & 17).

RICH VEGETABLE STOCK
MELTING CHEESE
VEGAN PARMESAN
JUST LIKE MAYO

Fridge basics

NUT & SEED BUTTER

PREP TIME 30 MINUTES
MAKES 1½ CUPS

Process 1 cup (160g) blanched roasted almonds, ½ cup (70g) roasted unsalted peanuts, ½ cup (75g) sunflower seeds, ¼ cup (40g) linseeds (flaxseeds), ½ cup (125ml) olive oil, 2 tablespoons pure maple syrup and ½ teaspoon sea salt flakes, in a high-powered blender, scraping down the sides regularly, for 5 minutes or until smooth. (For a less powerful blender it can take up to 20 minutes until the mixture reaches a smooth consistency.) Spoon butter into a jar; keep refrigerated for up to 3 weeks. Stir before using.

VEGAN CHIA PASTRY

PREP + COOK TIME 20 MINUTES (+ STANDING & REFRIGERATION)
MAKES ONE 24CM (9½IN) TART SHELL

Combine 1 tablespoon ground white chia seeds and ¼ cup (60ml) water in a small jug; stand for 30 minutes. Process 1⅔ cup (250g) plain (all-purpose) flour, 3 teaspoons caster (superfine) sugar, 1 teaspoon sea salt flakes, ½ cup (125ml) olive oil and 2 tablespoons soda water until mixture forms a dough. Shape into a disc; cover, refrigerate 30 minutes. Roll out pastry until large enough to line a 24cm (9½in) loose-based tart tin.

BETTA FETTA

PREP + COOK TIME 40 MINUTES (+ STANDING)
MAKES 1 CUP

Place ¾ cup (115g) raw cashews and ¾ cup (105g) raw macadamias in a bowl with enough water to cover; stand for 8 hours or overnight. Drain nuts; rinse well. Process nuts with 1 tablespoon nutritional yeast flakes, 1 teaspoon sea salt flakes, ¼ cup each lemon juice and extra virgin olive oil until smooth. Press firmly into a plastic-wrap-lined 9cm x 15cm (3¾in x 6in) container. Turn out onto a baking-paper-lined oven tray. Preheat oven to 200°C/400°F; bake for 20 minutes or until golden. Cool, cut into squares; store in olive oil with rosemary and thyme sprigs and garlic clove in the fridge for up 2 weeks.

ALMOND MYLK

PREP TIME 10 MINUTES (+ STANDING)
MAKES 3 CUPS

Place 1 cup (160g) natural almonds and a pinch of fine salt in a large bowl with enough cold water to cover; stand, covered, for 8 hours at room temperature in cool weather, or in the fridge during warm weather. Drain almonds; rinse well. Blend almonds with 3 cups (750ml) water until smooth. Pour mixture through a nut bag to release all the mylk. Store in a sealed glass bottle in the fridge for up to 3 days.

RICH VEGETABLE STOCK

PREP + COOK TIME 2½ HOURS
MAKES 2.5 LITRES (10 CUPS)

Coarsely chop 1 medium (350g) leek, 1 large (200g) unpeeled onion, 2 large (360g) carrots, 1 large (400g) swede, 2 celery stalks (with leaves) (300g) and 3 unpeeled cloves garlic. Place vegetables in a boiler with 1 teaspoon black peppercorns, 2 bay leaves, 2 sprigs each fresh rosemary, thyme and flat-leaf parsley and 5 litres (20 cups) water; bring to the boil. Reduce heat; simmer, for 2 hours. Strain stock through a sieve into a large bowl; discard solids. Cool. Store in the fridge for up to 3 days or freeze for up to 1 month.

MELTING CHEESE

PREP + COOK TIME 15 MINUTES (+ STANDING)
MAKES 900G (3¾ CUPS)

Place ½ cup (75g) raw cashews in a small bowl with enough water to cover; stand for 4 hours or overnight. Drain cashews; rinse well. In a blender, blend cashews, ½ cup (70g) raw macadamias, 3 cups (750ml) water, ⅔ cup (100g) arrowroot, ¼ cup (60ml) grape seed oil, ¼ cup (25g) nutritional yeast flakes, 2 teaspoons sea salt flakes and 2 tablespoons lemon juice until smooth. Stir mixture in a saucepan over medium heat for 8 minutes or until thick and stretchy like melted cheese. Cool. Store in an airtight container in the fridge for up to 2 weeks. Use in toasted sandwiches, nachos or pizzas.

VEGAN PARMESAN

PREP TIME 10 MINUTES
MAKES 1 CUP

Process ¾ cup (115g) raw cashews, ⅓ cup (25g) nutritional yeast flakes, ¾ teaspoon sea salt flakes and ¼ teaspoon garlic powder into a fine meal, similar in consistency to finely grated parmesan cheese. Store in an airtight container in the fridge for up to 2 months. Use as you would regular parmesan.

JUST LIKE MAYO

PREP TIME 5 MINUTES
MAKES 1 CUP

Drain liquid (aquafaba) from a 400g (12½oz) can chickpeas (garbanzo beans). Reserve ¼ cup (60ml) aquafaba; store leftover aquafaba in the fridge for up to 2 days. Blend reserved ¼ cup aquafaba with 1 tablespoon apple cider vinegar, ½ teaspoon sea salt flakes and ½ teaspoon dijon mustard in a small blender (do not use a food processor) until smooth. With the motor operating, add ½ cup (125ml) olive oil in a slow, steady stream until thick and creamy (mayo will also thicken in the fridge). Spoon mayo into a screw-top jar. Store in the fridge for up to 2 weeks.

WAKE UP

PREP + COOK TIME 15 MINUTES **SERVES** 2

TURMERIC TOFU SCRAMBLE

Tofu is an excellent source of calcium, and a 100g serving of tofu will provide you with 8g protein!

- **250g (8oz) firm tofu**
- **2 teaspoons nutritional yeast flakes (optional) (see tip)**
- **½ teaspoon ground turmeric**
- **½ teaspoon cumin seeds**
- **¼ teaspoon smoked paprika**
- **1 tablespoon water**
- **2 tablespoons extra virgin olive oil**
- **4 green onions (scallions), sliced thinly**
- **1 clove garlic, crushed**
- **1 tablespoon coarsely chopped fresh flat-leaf parsley**
- **1 tablespoon lemon juice**
- **4 bagels (169g), split, toasted**
- **⅓ cup (85g) chipotle hummus (see food swaps)**
- **2 medium tomatoes (300g), sliced**
- **50g (1½oz) baby spinach leaves**
- **½ cup snow pea tendrils**

1 Pat tofu dry with paper towel to remove excess moisture. Crumble tofu into a small bowl, using your hands.

2 Combine nutritional yeast, turmeric, cumin seeds, paprika and the water in a small bowl; season with salt and pepper.

3 Heat oil in a medium frying pan over medium-high heat; cook green onion and garlic for 1 minute or until softened. Add crumbled tofu; cook, stirring, for 4 minutes or until tofu starts to brown a little. Add the spice mixture; cook, stirring, for 1 minute or until tofu is completely coated. Stir in parsley and lemon juice until combined.

4 Spread toasted bagel halves with hummus; top bases with tomato, scrambled tofu, spinach leaves and snow pea tendrils.

tip Nutrional yeast flakes are a seasoning used to provide a moreish cheese-like umami taste. Look for a brand that is fortified with B12, a vitamin that can only be found in meat therefore needs to be supplemented on a vegan diet.

food swaps To add a smoky flavour to the scrambled tofu use smoked tofu, available from combined greengrocer delis and delis. You could also use other spicy, flavoured hummus, like jalapeño hummus or harissa hummus. Top with other greens such as rocket and watercress.

PREP + COOK TIME 15 MINUTES **SERVES** 2

AVOCADO TOAST WITH SMOKY CHICKPEAS

Save the drained liquid from the chickpeas (aquafaba) to make the Just Like Mayo, page 17.

- **1 cup (190g) drained canned chickpeas (garbanzo beans), rinsed**
- **2 tablespoons extra virgin olive oil**
- **½ teaspoon sea salt flakes**
- **½ teaspoon smoked paprika**
- **½ teaspoon ground cumin**
- **4 slices wholegrain sourdough bread (45g), toasted**
- **1 large avocado (320g), mashed**
- **⅓ cup micro herbs (see tip)**
- **2 tablespoons sriracha**
- **lime wedges, to serve**

1 Pat chickpeas dry with paper towel. Heat oil in a large frying pan over high heat; cook chickpeas and salt, stirring occasionally, for 5 minutes. Add paprika and cumin; cook, stirring, for a further 30 seconds.

2 Spread sourdough toast with mashed avocado. Top with smoky chickpeas and micro herbs; drizzle with sriracha. Serve with lime wedges.

tip You can use micro parsley or coriander, or any full-sized chopped soft-leaf herb such as flat-leaf parsley, dill, coriander (cilantro) or mint.

vegan hacks If you have leftover canned chickpeas, reserve them for the loaded sweet potatoes with chickpea tabbouleh, page 83.

PREP + COOK TIME 20 MINUTES MAKES 2

NO-EGG SPINACH & TOMATO OMELETTE

Making your own vegan fetta is delicious and easy. To learn how, see our Betta Fetta, page 16.

- 300g (9½oz) silken tofu
- 2 tablespoons extra virgin olive oil
- ⅓ cup (80ml) soy milk
- ⅓ cup (50g) chickpea flour (besan)
- 2 tablespoons nutritional yeast flakes
- ½ teaspoon sea salt flakes
- ¼ teaspoon ground turmeric

SPINACH FILLING

- 120g (4oz) spinach leaf salad mix
- 1 shallot, sliced thinly
- 200g (6½oz) heirloom cherry tomatoes, sliced or halved
- 1 tablespoon red wine vinegar
- 2 tablespoons extra virgin olive oil
- 60g (2oz) drained marinated vegan fetta (see vegan hacks)

1 Pat tofu dry with paper towel. Blend tofu with 1 tablespoon of the oil and remaining ingredients in a blender until smooth.

2 Heat a 22cm (9in) non-stick frying pan over high heat. Add 2 teaspoons of the oil; reduce heat to medium-high. Add half the tofu mixture; swirl or spread mixture until base is covered; cook for 3 minutes or until small bubbles appear on surface. Slide omelette onto a warm plate; cover to keep warm. Repeat with remaining oil and tofu mixture to make a second omelette; slide onto a second warm plate.

3 Make spinach filling.

4 Divide filling between omelettes, placing it over half of each omelette; fold over. Serve immediately.

spinach filling Place leaves, shallot, tomatoes, vinegar and oil in a medium bowl; toss gently to combine. Top with fetta.

vegan hacks There are various nut-based vegan fettas available in the market place to choose from. Our favourite is made from macadamias. You could also use other vegan cheeses or crumbled tofu or tempeh.

A healthy start

SUPER SEED BIRCHER

PREP TIME 15 MINUTES (+ REFRIGERATION) **SERVES** 4

Crumble ½ cup coconut flakes into a medium bowl. Stir in ⅓ cup sunflower seeds, ⅓ cup pepitas (pumpkin seed kernels), ¼ cup white chia seeds, ¼ cup flaxseed meal and 1¼ cups almond milk; cover, refrigerate for at least 1 hour or overnight. Cut 2 medium (300g) green apples into matchsticks and thickly slice 200g (6oz) strawberries. Divide seed mixture among bowls; top with apple and strawberry. Drizzle with coconut nectar syrup or pure maple syrup.

POMEGRANATE & PEAR BIRCHER

PREP TIME 15 MINUTES (+ REFRIGERATION) **SERVES** 6

Combine 2 cups almond milk and 1 cup pomegranate juice in a medium bowl. Add 1 cup rolled oats, ½ cup quinoa flakes and 2 tablespoons white chia seeds; stir to combine. Grate 1 large (330g) pear, add to oat mixture; stir to combine. Cover; refrigerate for 3 hours or overnight. Divide bircher among bowls, drizzle with pure maple syrup. Top each serving with 1 tablesoon pomegranate seeds, 2 slices pear and a little grated orange rind.

tip Pomegrante seeds (arils) are sold in small punnets in the fresh food section at supermarkets.

COCONUT TROPICAL BIRCHER

PREP TIME 15 MINUTES **SERVES** 4

Combine 3 cups quinoa flakes, 1 cup coconut milk, 1 cup coconut water and 1 cup cloudy apple juice in a medium bowl. Divide bircher among four bowls. Cut 1 small (250g) dragon fruit and 1 small (300g) mango into slices; divide fruit among bowls. Serve bircher topped with the pulp of 1 passionfruit and ¼ cup coconut flakes.

MAKE-AND-GO BIRCHER

PREP TIME 10 MINUTES **SERVES** 2

Cut 1 large (230g) ripe banana in half. Place each half in a 2-cup (500ml) glass jar; mash with a fork. Cut 1 large (200g) red apple with the skin on into matchsticks; divide between jars. Add ½ cup rolled oats and a pinch of ground cinnamon. Top each jar with 1 tablespoon pepitas (pumpkin seed kernels) and 2 tablespoons blueberries. Stir ¾ cup almond and coconut milk into each jar. Seal and go.

PREP + COOK TIME 20 MINUTES (+ STANDING) **SERVES** 2

CHOCOLATE PANCAKES WITH MAPLE BANANA

Dutch-processed cocoa is treated with an alkalising ingredient to neutralise cocoa's naturally acidic taste.

- **2 tablespoons vegetable oil**
- **2 small bananas (260g)**
- **2 tablespoons pure maple syrup, plus extra to serve**
- **½ cup (140g) coconut yoghurt**
- **100g (3oz) fresh cherries**

PANCAKE BATTER

- **1¼ cup (185g) self-raising flour**
- **2 tablespoons dutch-processed cocoa**
- **½ teaspoon bicarbonate of soda (baking soda)**
- **½ teaspoon ground cinnamon**
- **¾ cup (180ml) almond milk**
- **2 teaspoons apple cider vinegar**
- **⅓ cup (80ml) pure maple syrup**

1 Make pancake batter.

2 Heat a large, non-stick frying pan over medium heat; brush with a little oil. Pour ¼-cups of the pancake batter into pan; cook pancakes, in batches, for 2 minutes or until bubbles appear on the surface. Turn pancakes; cook for a further 1 minute or until lightly browned. Remove from pan; cover to keep warm. Repeat with remaining oil and batter to make 8 pancakes in total. Reserve pan.

3 Slice bananas on a sharp angle. Place reserved pan over medium-high heat. Add maple syrup and bananas to hot pan; cook for 2 minutes or until caramelised, turn and cook for a further 30 seconds.

4 Serve pancakes topped with coconut yoghurt, caramelised bananas, cherries and extra syrup.

pancake batter Sift flour, cocoa, bicarbonate of soda and cinnamon into a medium bowl. Whisk milk, vinegar and maple syrup together in a small jug. Make a well in the centre of flour. Gradually pour in almond milk mixture, while whisking until a smooth batter forms; stand for 5 minutes.

food swap Use your favourite berries instead of cherries.

keep it Pancakes can be frozen for up to 1 month.

PREP TIME 20 MINUTES **SERVES** 2

UNICORN CHIA PARFAITS

Unicorn food is fantastical natural pastel-coloured Instagramable food. Join in the fun here.

- **⅓ cup (55g) black chia seeds**
- **1⅓ cups (330ml) almond milk**
- **½ teaspoon vanilla extract**
- **1½ cups (420g) coconut yoghurt, plus extra to serve**
- **1 teaspoon freeze-dried blueberry powder**
- **¼ teaspoon beetroot powder**
- **⅛ teaspoon spirulina powder**
- **1 medium banana (200g), sliced thinly**
- **200g (6½oz) seedless watermelon, sliced thinly**
- **edible flowers and flaked coconut, to serve**

1 Place chia seeds and 1 cup (250ml) of the almond milk in a medium bowl; whisk with a fork for 2 minutes or until chia seeds have absorbed the milk. Gradually stir in remaining almond milk and vanilla. Cover; refrigerate for 15 minutes or until mixture thickens.

2 Meanwhile, divide coconut yoghurt into three small bowls; stir blueberry powder into one, beetroot powder into the second and spirulina powder into the third.

3 Cut banana and watermelon slices into 3cm (1¼in) stars, using star cutters.

4 Divide blueberry yoghurt between two 2-cup (500ml) jars or glasses. Spoon half the chia mixture between jars; layer with beetroot yoghurt, remaining chia mixture and spirulina yoghurt. Top with a dollop of extra coconut yoghurt, the banana and watermelon stars, then edible flowers and flaked coconut.

vegan hacks Freeze-dried blueberry powder and beetroot powder are available from some health food stores, gourmet food stores, pharmacies and vitamin stores. Spiriluna is available from supermarkets and health food stores.

PREP + COOK TIME 35 MINUTES (+ FREEZING) **SERVES** 2

SAUSAGE & EGG MOCK MUFFIN

Serve the breakfast muffin as is or plated with sliced avocado, baby spinach leaves and hash browns.

- 2 tablespoons olive oil
- 1 large onion (200g), chopped finely
- 250g (8oz) packaged microwave short-grain brown rice
- 400g (12½oz) can black beans, drained, rinsed
- 1 teaspoon smoked paprika
- 1 teaspoon onion powder
- 1 teaspoon garlic powder
- 2 tablespoons barbecue sauce
- ¼ cup (35g) plain (all-purpose) flour, plus extra for dusting
- 300g (9½oz) silken tofu
- 2 tablespoons vegan mayonnaise
- ¼ teaspoon ground turmeric
- 2 english muffins (130g), split
- 2 tablespoons olive oil, extra
- 2 slices vegan cheddar (36g)
- tomato sauce (ketchup), to serve

1 Heat olive oil in a medium frying pan over high heat; cook onion, stirring frequently, for 5 minutes until browned. Transfer to a food processor with rice, beans, paprika, onion and garlic powders, barbecue sauce and flour; season. Pulse until mixture comes together.

2 Line a tray with plastic wrap. With damp hands, shape ⅓-cup amounts of mixture into six 8cm (3¼in) patties. Place on tray; freeze for 20 minutes or until firm (see tips).

3 Pat tofu dry with paper towel. Cut tofu in half horizontally to make two 1.5cm (¾in) thick slices. (Take care with cutting the tofu as it is fragile.) Using an 8cm (3¼in) cutter, carefully cut one round from each tofu slice, reserve offcuts (see vegan hacks). Combine vegan mayonnaise and turmeric in a small bowl.

4 Preheat grill (broiler) on high. Place muffin halves, cut-side up, on an oven tray; place under grill until lightly toasted.

5 Heat half the extra oil in a non-stick frying pan over medium heat. Lightly dust patties with extra flour. Cook patties for 3 minutes on each side or until browned. Top toasted muffin bases with patties and a slice of cheese; place under grill for 30 seconds or until melted.

6 Heat remaining oil in same pan; cook tofu rounds for 2 minutes on each side or until crisp and golden. Place on cheese-topped pattie.

7 Place a tablespoon of turmeric mayonnaise in the centre of each tofu round to resemble an egg yolk. Add tomato sauce to taste and top with muffin lid.

tip This recipe makes 6 patties but only uses 2 in these breakfast muffins; freeze the remaining 4 patties in an airtight container between sheets of baking paper for up to 2 months. To use, cook from frozen.

vegan hacks Tofu off cuts can be added to a fruit smoothie for an added protein hit.

ACTIVE VEGAN

PREP + COOK TIME 15 MINUTES **MAKES** 2½ CUPS

MAPLE & CAYENNE TRAIL MIX

The active ingredient in cayenne pepper, capsaicin, is used in traditional Chinese and Ayurvedic medicine.

- **1 cup (120g) pecans**
- **½ cup (100g) pepitas (pumpkin seed kernels)**
- **¼ cup (40g) sunflower seeds**
- **½ cup (35g) moist coconut flakes**
- **¼ cup (40g) sultanas**
- **1 tablespoon pure maple syrup**
- **1 teaspoon sea salt flakes**
- **¼ teaspoon cayenne pepper**

1 Preheat oven to 180°C/360°F. Line an oven tray with baking paper.

2 Place pecans, pepitas, sunflower seeds, coconut flakes and sultanas in a medium bowl. Add maple syrup, salt flakes and cayenne pepper; toss to coat well. Spread mixture evenly in a single layer on lined tray.

3 Bake nut mixture for 10 minutes, stirring halfway through cooking or until evenly golden. Cool.

food swaps Try ground cumin instead of cayenne pepper and cashews instead of pecans.

keep it Store trail mix in an airtight container for up to 2 weeks.

PREP TIME 20 MINUTES (+ REFRIGERATION) **MAKES** 16 BARS

IRON POWER BARS

Tahini, molasses, prunes and spirulina all contain adequate amounts of plant-based iron for vegans.

- **1 cup (170g) pitted prunes**
- **¼ cup (70g) tahini**
- **⅓ cup (75g) coconut oil, melted**
- **2 tablespoons molasses**
- **1½ cups (180g) almond meal**
- **1 tablespoon cacao powder**
- **1 teaspoon spirulina powder (optional)**
- **2 tablespoons finely chopped pistachios**

1 Grease a 12cm x 25cm (4¾in x 10in) (base measurement) loaf pan; line with baking paper.

2 Process prunes until it forms a paste. Add tahini, coconut oil and molasses; process briefly until just combined. Add almond meal, cacao and spirulina powders; process until well combined.

3 Spoon mixture into loaf pan; press level along the base until approximately 1cm (½in) thick. Sprinkle with pistachios; press pistachios into surface using your fingers. Refrigerate for at least 1 hour or until firm.

4 Remove from loaf pan. Trim edges; cut into 16 bars crossways.

tip For a less substantial snack, cut the mixture into 3cm (1¼in) squares for iron power bites (you will get 28), or roll tablespoons of the mixture for bliss balls, increasing the amount of pistachios to coat.

vegan hacks Spiriluna is obtained from blue green algae; it is high in antioxidants, contains anti-inflammatory properties and according to research has anti-cancer properties. It is available from supermarkets and health food stores.

keep it Store bars in an airtight container in the fridge for up to 2 weeks or freeze for up to 1 month.

PREP TIME 10 MINUTES **MAKES** 2½ CUPS

ORANGE & VANILLA RAWNOLA

Shop for fresh plump medjool dates from the fresh food section of supermarkest to make this recipe.

- 1 cup (90g) rolled oats
- 12 fresh dates (240g), pitted
- ½ cup (40g) shredded coconut
- 2 teaspoons finely grated orange rind
- 1 teaspoon vanilla bean paste

1 Place ingredients in a food processor; pulse until they start to clump together. (Do not over-process or the mixture will form a ball.)

2 Transfer rawnola to an airtight container. Store in the fridge for up to 2 weeks.

serving ideas Serve the rawnola on its own as a snack or for something more substantial serve with vegan yoghurt, stone fruit and berries.

vegan hacks For bliss balls, process the mixture until it comes together then roll tablespoons of mixture into balls.

FLAVOUR VARIATIONS

fig + almond rawnola Swap dried dates for figs and almonds for coconut.

apricot + walnut rawnola Swap dried dates with apricots and walnuts for coconut.

apple + brazil nut rawnola Swap dates for dried apple and brazil nuts for coconut.

Boost & recovery drinks

STRONG BONES

PREP TIME 5 MINUTES **SERVES** 2

Grate 1 teaspoon of rind from 1 large (300g) orange; squeeze juice. Blend rind and juice with 1 cup (250ml) almond milk, 2 small (100g) fresh figs, chopped, 1 tablespoon vanilla vegan protein powder (see vegan hacks), 1 tablespoon tahini and 1 tablespoon white chia seeds in a high-powered blender until smooth. Serve in jars or glasses with extra thinly sliced fresh figs pressed to the inside of the jar, if you like, topped with 2 teaspoons freeze-dried raspberries.

vegan hacks Many protein powders are whey based. On a vegan diet you require a plant-based protein powder made from either pea or brown rice protein, available from health food stores.

CHOC SPICE SLUSHIE

PREP TIME 10 MINUTES (+ FREEZING) **SERVES** 2

Place 2 large (460g) chopped bananas in an airtight container or resealable plastic bag. Freeze for 4 hours or until firm. Blend frozen banana with 1½ cups (375ml) almond milk, 1 tablespoon cacao powder, 1 tablespoon chia seeds, 1 tablespoon tahini and ½ teaspoon ground cardamom in a high-powered blender until smooth. Serve immediately dusted with cacao powder and topped with pieces of vegan chocolate, if you like.

tip To create a striped affect in your serving glass, blend 2 teaspoons cacoa powder and 1 tablespoon honey to form a paste. Spread paste on the inside of each glass.

POST-RUN REFRESHER

PREP TIME 5 MINUTES **SERVES** 2

Push 1 telegraph (400g) unpeeled, coarsely chopped cucumber, 1 baby cos (romaine) lettuce (300g) coarsely chopped, 2 medium (460g) unpeeled coarsely chopped pears and ½ medium (70g) peeled lemon through a juice extractor, into a jug. Stir in 1 cup (250ml) chilled coconut water. Serve immediately over ice.

tips The juice will separate on standing, however a quick stir will bring it back together. Swap the pear for apple for a variation.

ORANGE & VANILLA BEAN COCONUT WATER

PREP TIME 5 MINUTES (+ REFRIGERATION)
MAKES 1 LITRE (4 CUPS)

Using a vegetable peeler, peel rind from 1 small (190g) navel orange into long wide strips, avoiding any white pith. Squeeze juice. Place orange rind and juice in a large jug with 1 litre (4 cups) coconut water and 1 vanilla bean, split lengthways; stir to combine. Refrigerate for 1 hour or until chilled.

tip The water will keep in the refrigerator for up to 48 hours.

PREP + COOK TIME 35 MINUTES **MAKES** 20

KING KONG COOKIES

Just like their name sake suggest, these monster cookies will tide you over until your next big meal.

- **2 medium bananas (400g)**
- **2½ cups (225g) rolled oats**
- **1 cup (75g) shredded coconut**
- **½ cup (70g) roasted salted peanuts, chopped coarsely**
- **⅓ cup (35g) cacao powder, sifted**
- **½ cup (125ml) pure maple syrup**
- **¼ cup (60ml) extra virgin olive oil**
- **8 fresh dates (160g), pitted, chopped finely**
- **¼ cup (35g) cacao nibs (see vegan hacks)**

1 Preheat oven to 180°C/350°F. Line two oven trays with baking paper.

2 Mash bananas in a large bowl until smooth; you will need ¾ cup mashed banana. Add remaining ingredients, except cacao nibs, to the bowl; using clean hands, mix until well combined.

3 Using damp hands, roll heaped tablespoons of mixture into balls. Place on trays; flatten slightly to 6cm (2½in) rounds (cookies will not spread). Sprinkle with cacao nibs.

4 Bake cookies for 20 minutes or until golden brown on the outside. Cool on trays.

keep it Store cookies in an airtight container at room temperature for up to 3 days or freeze in airtight bags for up to 1 month.

vegan hacks Cacao nibs are fermented crushed dried cacao beans. When they are ground to a liquor they become the starting point for making chocolate, before sugar and milk is added. They are available from major supermarkets and health food stores.

PREP + COOK TIME 55 MINUTES MAKES 8 THICK SLICES

BANANA & HEMP SEED BREAD

Super nutritious hemp seeds have a pleasant nutty taste, a little like a mix of hazelnuts and almonds.

- **4 medium ripe bananas (800g)**
- **¾ cup (165g) firmly packed brown sugar**
- **¾ cup (170g) coconut oil, melted, cooled**
- **1 teaspoon vanilla bean paste**
- **1¾ cups (280g) wholemeal plain (all-purpose) flour**
- **¼ cup (35g) plain (all-purpose) flour**
- **1 teaspoon ground cinnamon**
- **½ teaspoon ground nutmeg**
- **2 teaspoons baking powder**
- **1 teaspoon bicarbonate of soda (baking soda)**
- **1 teaspoon sea salt flakes**
- **⅓ cup (45g) hemp seeds**
- **2 small ripe bananas (260g), extra**
- **1 tablespoon pure maple syrup**

1 Preheat oven to 180°C/350°F. Grease a 12cm x 22cm (4¾in x 8¾in) loaf pan; line base and sides with baking paper, extending the paper 2cm (¾in) above the edge.

2 Mash medium bananas in a large bowl until smooth; you will need 1½ cups (420g) mashed banana. Add sugar; mash until combined. Whisk in coconut oil and vanilla until well combined.

3 Sift flours, spices, baking powder, bicarbonate of soda and salt over banana mixture; add husks to the bowl. Gently fold dry ingredients into banana mixture, then stir in ¼ cup of the hemp seeds. Spoon banana mixture into pan; sprinkle with remaining hemp seeds. Cut small bananas in half lengthways; place, cut-side up, on mixture, then brush with maple syrup.

4 Bake loaf for 45 minutes or until a skewer inserted into the centre comes out clean. Leave in the pan for 5 minutes before turning, top-side up, onto a wire rack to cool completely.

tip Cut banana bread into thick slices and place into zip-top sandwich bags ready to go or freeze for up to 2 months.

vegan hacks Hemp seeds are low in THC, the hallucinogenic substance found in marijuana, and do not induce a high. It is a nutritious seed with the perfect natural mix of omega-3 and omega-6 fatty acids. As well, it is a complete protein source containing all nine essential amino acids and is rich in muscle-building leucine. They are available from health food stores.

serving ideas Serve with vanilla fluff (page 142), fresh raspberries, edible flowers and pure maple syrup.

PREP TIME 20 MINUTES **SERVES** 2

BANANA & CASHEW BUTTER

You can also try the cashew butter spread on cross sections of apple, pear or persimmon.

- **2 tablespoons natural flaked almonds**
- **2 tablespoons sunflower seeds**
- **2 tablespoons flaked coconut**
- **1 tablespoon white sesame seeds**
- **½ teaspoon ground cinnamon**
- **1½ tablespoons rice malt syrup**
- **2 small bananas (260g), halved lengthways**
- **2 teaspoons rice malt syrup, extra**

CASHEW BUTTER

- **2 cups (300g) raw cashews**

1 Make cashew butter.

2 Place almonds, sunflower seeds, coconut, sesame seeds and cinnamon in a small frying pan, stirring continuously over medium heat, for 2 minutes or until lightly browned. Add rice malt syrup; stir continuously, for 1 minute or until browned. Transfer to a small baking-paper-lined tray. Leave to cool slightly, then break into pieces.

3 Spread 1 tablespoon of cashew butter over each banana half, drizzle with extra rice malt syrup and sprinkle with toasted seed mix.

cashew butter Process cashews, scraping down the side of the bowl regularly, for 10-15 minutes or until completely smooth (see tips). (Makes 1 cup)

tips Powerful commercial food processors will take about 10 minutes to process the cashew butter, while small retail home-use processors may take longer. If yours is taking a long time, add 2 tablespoons hot water to loosen the mixture. The trick to nut butter is to keep processing but give the machine a break occasionally, so it doesn't over heat.

keep it Nut butter will keep in an airtight container for up to 1 month. In summer, it is best stored in the fridge.

food swap If you prefer you can use a commercially made cashew butter or even crunchy peanut butter.

Recovery mineral salts

RECOVERY BATH SALTS

PREP TIME 5 MINUTES **MAKES** ENOUGH FOR 1 BATH

Combine 2 cups epsom salts (magnesium sulfate) and 2 tablespoons bicarbonate of soda (baking soda) in a small bowl. Add 4 drops of rosemary or lavender essential oils. You can also add fresh sprigs of rosemary or lavender. To use, fill a bath tub with warm-hot water. Add epsom salt mix; stir with your hands to dissolve crystals. Soak in the bath for 15 minutes. To increase the benefits of the soak, use a body brush to open up the skins pores. Avoid swallowing the water as the high magnesium content can result in a laxative effect. Not suitable for children or pregnant women.

CHAMOMILE RELAXING SOAK

PREP TIME 5 MINUTES **MAKES** ENOUGH FOR 1 BATH

Combine 2 cups epsom salts (magnesium sulfate) and 2 tablespoons bicarbonate of soda (baking soda) in a small bowl. Add 4 drops of chamomile essential oil. You can also add a handful of dried chamomile flowers. To use, fill a bath tub with warm-hot water. Add epsom salt mix; stir with your hands to dissolve crystals. Soak in the bath for 15 minutes. To increase the benefits of the soak, use a body brush to open up the skins pores. Avoid swallowing the water as the high magnesium content can result in a laxative effect. Not suitable for children or pregnant women.

Bathing in mineral salts aids muscle recovery through immersive heat therapy and absorption of magnesium through the skin, to replenish depleted stores from exercise induced electrolyte loss. Epsom salts are both inexpensive and readily available from chemists and supermarkets.

PEPPERMINT FOOT SOAK

PREP TIME 5 MINUTES **MAKES** ENOUGH FOR 1 SOAK

Place ½ cup epsom salts (magnesium sulfate) and 4 drops of peppermint essential oil in a large bowl of warm water. Soak your feet in the water for 20 minutes. You can use a pumice stone to work away any dead skin. Dry your feet well then moisturise with a rich moisturiser. Not suitable for pregnant women.

tip Pumice stones are made from a light-weight hardened lava foam. They are available from chemists.

DOUGHNUT BATH BOMBS

PREP TIME 10 MINUTES (+ 24 HOURS STANDING)
MAKES 6

Sift ½ cup bicarbonate of soda (baking soda), ⅓ cup citric acid, ½ cup epsom salts (magnesium sulfate) and ½ cup cornflour (cornstarch) into a medium bowl. Combine ⅓ cup olive oil and 1 teaspoon rose oil (or your favourite essential oil) in a small jug. Pour wet ingredients over dry; using your hands, combine until mixture starts to clump. Divide 2 tablespoons dried rose petals (or dried herbs) among a 6-hole (¼ cup/60ml) silicon doughnut mould (or use a mini muffin pan), then spoon in mixture. Stand for 24 hours to dry, pressing down firmly again after a few hours. Bombs will keep for up 2 weeks. Add bath bombs to a bath of warm water, just before getting in.

PREP TIME 10 MINUTES **SERVES** 2

EAT THE RAINBOW AVOCADO HALVES

For one person you can halve the recipe, or double the recipe ingredients for 4 people (as pictured).

- **1 large avocado (320g), halved**
- **½ small carrot (35g), julienned or grated (see tip)**
- **½ small beetroot (beet) (50g), julienned or grated (see tip)**
- **2 tablespoons kimchi**
- **1 tablespoon sprouts (optional)**

LEMON TAHINI DRESSING

- **1 tablespoon tahini**
- **1½ tablespoons water**
- **1 tablespoon lemon juice**
- **2 teaspoons extra virgin olive oil**

1 Make lemon tahini dressing.

2 Place avocado halves on a plate; fill each half with carrot, beetroot and kimchi. Drizzle with dressing and top with sprouts; season.

lemon tahini dressing Stir ingredients in a small bowl until well combined.

tip A julienne peeler looks like a wide-bladed vegetable peeler with a serrated, rather than straight blade. They are available from kitchenware stores and Asian grocers. Alternatively, you can cut the carrot and beetroot into julienne (matchsticks), using a mandoline or sharp knife.

OUT & ABOUT

PREP + COOK TIME 35 MINUTES **SERVES** 2

MEXICAN QUINOA POTS

Make the pots with white, red or tri-coloured quinoa, or other wholegrains, like barley or farro.

- ½ cup (100g) white quinoa, rinsed
- 1 corn cob (250g), husks and silks removed
- 400g (12½oz) can black beans, drained, rinsed
- 1 small red capsicum (bell pepper) (150g), chopped finely
- 2 green onions (scallions), sliced thinly
- 1½ tablespoons extra virgin olive oil
- 2 tablespoons lime juice
- 1 fresh long red chilli, sliced thinly
- 1 small avocado (200g)
- 1 small clove garlic, crushed
- 2 fresh coriander (cilantro) sprigs
- 2 lime wedges
- corn chips, to serve (optional)

1 Place quinoa and 2 cups (500ml) water in a small saucepan over medium-high heat; bring to the boil. Reduce heat to low; simmer for 12 minutes or until tender. Drain; rinse under cold water.

2 Heat a chargrill pan (or heavy-based frying pan) over high heat. Cook corn, rotating on all sides for 12 minutes or until lightly charred. Cool slightly; cut kernels from cob.

3 Place cooked quinoa and corn kernels in a medium bowl with black beans, capsicum, green onion, olive oil, half the lime juice and halve the chilli; stir to combine. Season to taste.

4 Place avocado, garlic and remaining lime juice in a small bowl; mash to combine. Season to taste.

5 To assemble jars, spoon quinoa mixture in the base of two 3-cup (750ml) jars. Top with guacamole, coriander sprigs, remaining chilli and a lime wedge. Serve with corn chips.

tip The salads can be assembled in any container you prefer.

food swaps You can use canned red kidney beans instead of black beans.

PREP + COOK TIME 30 MINUTES **SERVES** 2

SAMOSA WRAPS

Mix it up by using orange sweet potato and different varieties of wraps and chutney.

- **1 large potato (300g), peeled, cut into 1cm (½in) pieces**
- **2 tablespoons extra virgin olive oil**
- **½ cup (60g) frozen peas**
- **2 teaspoons curry powder**
- **2 red quinoa wraps (90g)**
- **2 tablespoons vegan mayonnaise (just like mayo, see page 17)**
- **30g (1oz) baby spinach leaves**
- **1 lebanese cucumber (130g), thinly sliced lengthways**
- **½ small red onion (50g), sliced thinly**
- **⅓ cup fresh coriander (cilantro)**
- **2 tablespoons mango chutney**
- **½ medium lime (45g), cut into wedges**

1 Boil, steam or microwave potato until just tender; drain.

2 Heat oil in a medium frying pan over high heat; cook potato, peas and curry powder, stirring, for 3 minutes or until potatoes are slightly mashed and peas are hot.

3 Spread wraps with mayonnaise, top with spinach leaves, cucumber, onion, coriander, potato mixture and chutney. Roll up to enclose filling. Serve with lime wedges.

tips These wraps can be enjoyed warm or cold. For cold wraps, allow potato filling to cool before assembling. Cover assembled wraps in plastic wrap and refrigerate until ready to eat. If you would like to eat these warm but are making them ahead of time, keep the filling and wraps separate; warm the potato filling just before assembling and eating. The potato mixture will keep refrigerated for up to 3 days.

PREP + COOK TIME 45 MINUTES SERVES 2

CARROT & MILLET PATTIES WITH SUNFLOWER SLAW

Millet is a nutrient dense small seed packed with fibre, protein, several B vitamins and minerals.

- 1 cup (250ml) vegetable stock
- ½ cup (100g) millet
- 1 shallot, chopped finely
- ⅓ cup (50g) chopped sun-dried tomatoes, chopped finely
- 1 medium carrot (120g), grated finely
- 1 tablespoon tomato paste
- 1 tablespoon fresh lemon juice
- lemon wedges, to serve

SUNFLOWER SLAW

- 2 tablespoons fresh lemon juice
- ¼ cup (60ml) extra virgin olive oil
- 2 teaspoons dijon mustard
- 2 cups (160g) finely shredded green cabbage
- 1 cup (80g) finely shredded red cabbage
- ½ cup fresh mint leaves
- ¼ cup (40g) sunflower seeds

1 Preheat oven 200°C/400°F. Line an oven tray with baking paper.

2 Bring stock to the boil in a small saucepan. Reduce heat to low; partially cover with a lid.

3 Stir millet in a medium saucepan over medium heat for 3 minutes or until fragrant and toasted. Add hot stock to millet, stir well. Bring to the boil. Reduce heat to low; cook millet, covered, for 15 minutes or until liquid is absorbed.

4 Transfer millet to a food processor. Add shallot, sun-dried tomato, carrot, tomato paste and lemon juice. Season. Pulse until mixture comes together but still has some texture.

5 Shape ¼ cups of millet mixture into four 8cm (3¼in) patties; place on lined tray. Bake for 20 minutes or until golden and crisp.

6 Make sunflower slaw.

7 Serve patties with slaw.

sunflower slaw Blend lemon juice, oil and mustard in a blender until smooth. Season to taste. Place cabbages, mint and 2 tablespoons of the seeds in a medium bowl with the dressing; toss well to combine. Sprinkle with remaining seeds.

do-ahead You can make the dressing, shred the cabbage, shape the patties (or even bake the patties), a day ahead. Store each ingredient separately in the fridge. Reheat the patties before serving.

serving ideas Serve with vegan mayonnaise (just like mayo, page 17) blended with 2 tablespoons coarsely chopped mint leaves and 2 teaspoons lemon juice.

Work snacks

MISO SNACK MIX

PREP + COOK TIME 35 MINUTES **MAKES** 3¾ CUPS

Preheat oven to 140°C/280°F. Line two oven trays with baking paper. Combine 2 cups raw cashews, 1 cup brazil nuts, 1½ cups peanuts, ½ cup pepitas (pumpkin seed kernels), ⅓ cup sunflower seeds, 1 teaspoon chilli flakes, 2 tablespoons white (shiro) miso and 2 teaspoons each sesame oil and peanut oil in a bowl until well coated. Spread mixture between trays. Roast for 30 minutes, stirring half way through, or until golden. Cool. Stir through ½ cup sultanas. Transfer to a zip-top bag or airtight container. Keeps for up to 1 month.

APRICOT & COCONUT BALLS

PREP TIME 15 MINUTES **MAKES** 24

Process 2⅔ cups dried apricots, 1 cup almond meal, 2 cups desiccated coconut, 2 cups unsalted roasted cashews, ½ cup rolled oats, 2 tablespoons white chia seeds, ¼ cup coconut yoghurt, 1 teaspoon finely grated orange rind, 1 teaspoon vanilla extract, 2 tablespoons lemon juice and 2 tablespoons rice bran syrup until well combined or until mixture clumps together and starts to clean the side of the bowl. Shape mixture into 24 balls; roll in ⅓ cup extra desiccated coconut to coat. Place on a tray, cover; refrigerate for 1 hour or until chilled. Transfer to an airtight container. Keeps refrigerated for up to 3 weeks.

Whether you are at work or at play when energy levels slump, nourishing snacks can make all the difference between happiness and irritability.

CAULIFLOWER HUMMUS

PREP + COOK TIME 35 MINUTES **MAKES** 3½ CUPS

Preheat oven to 200°C/400°F. Line a large oven tray with baking paper. Place 1 small (1kg) cauliflower, cut into florets on tray with 3 cloves garlic. Drizzle with 1 tablespoon extra virgin olive oil; season. Roast for 25 minutes or until tender. Cool. Process cauliflower, garlic, 400g (12½oz) can drained and rinsed chickpeas (garbanzo beans), ⅓ cup cashew spread and ¼ cup lemon juice until smooth. With motor running, add ¼ cup extra virgin olive oil until combined. Season. Refrigerate until needed. Fold in 45g (1½oz) dukkah before serving. Serve with baby carrots, cucumber, celery sticks and radishes for dipping. Keeps refrigerated for up to 3 days.

SEEDED CRISPBREADS

PREP + COOK TIME 55 MINUTES (+ COOLING) **MAKES** 24

Place a large oven tray in the oven, then preheat to 180°C/350°F. Combine 30g (1oz) chia seeds and ½ cup water in a small bowl; soak for 10 minutes. Pulse 1 cup sunflower seeds and ½ cup pepitas (pumpkin seed kernels) in a food processor until finely chopped; transfer to a large bowl. Stir in ½ cup buckwheat flour and ¼ cup dukkah. Add soaked chia and ¼ cup melted coconut oil; season with salt. Using your hands, mix then shape into a ball. Roll dough between two sheets of baking paper to a 23cm x 33cm (9¼in x 13¼in) rectangle. Score into 24 rectangles. Using baking paper, lift onto preheated tray. Bake for 25 minutes or until crisp and lightly brown. Cut while still warm. Cool. Keeps for up to 2 weeks.

PREP + COOK TIME 50 MINUTES **MAKES** 12

ZUCCHINI & KALE FRITTATAS

Turmeric and ginger are both powerful anti-inflammatories that aid in the digestion of fats.

- **4 medium zucchini (480g)**
- **2 tablespoons extra virgin olive oil**
- **1 medium onion (150g), chopped finely**
- **½ teaspoon cumin seeds, crushed**
- **½ teaspoon fennel seeds, crushed**
- **2 cloves garlic, crushed**
- **2 tablespoons grated fresh ginger**
- **350g (11oz) purple kale**
- **300g (9½oz) firm tofu, drained of excess liquid**
- **½ cup (125ml) soy milk**
- **⅓ cup (55g) wholemeal plain (all-purpose) flour**
- **2 tablespoons nutritional yeast flakes**
- **1 teaspoon ground turmeric**
- **olive oil cooking spray**

1 Preheat oven to 160°C/325°F. Grease a 12-hole (⅓ cup/80ml) muffin pan; line bases and sides with overlapping squares of baking paper.

2 Coarsely grate 3 of the zucchini; place in the middle of a piece of muslin then wring out excess liquid. (Alternatively, pick up small handfuls of zucchini and squeeze tightly to remove excess liquid.)

3 Heat oil in a frying pan over medium heat; cook onion and seeds, stirring, for 4 minutes or until onion softens. Add garlic and ginger; cook for a further minute or until fragrant.

4 Strip the kale leaves from the stem; discard stems. You will need 200g (6½oz). Coarsely chop two-thirds of the kale leaves. Add chopped kale and grated zucchini to the pan; cook for a further 2 minutes. Cool.

5 Meanwhile, process tofu, soy milk, flour, nutritional yeast and turmeric in a food processor until smooth.

6 Combine tofu mixture and zucchini mixture in a large jug. Pour mixture into pan holes. Using a vegetable peeler, peel remaining zucchini into long thin ribbons. Roll up ribbons; top frittatas with remaining kale leaves and zucchini rolls. Spray with cooking oil spray.

7 Bake frittatas for 20 minutes or until golden and firm.

food swap Instead of the kale, use the same weight of cavolo nero (tuscan kale), which is a straight-leafed form of kale.

serving idea Serve with vegan mayonnaise (just like mayo, page 17).

vegan hack Leafy greens provide the vegan eater with an arsenal of nutrients – iron, calcium and an array of valuable vitamins. Increase your iron absorption by serving the frittatas with a wedge of lemon.

PREP TIME 10 MINUTES **SERVES** 1

CRUNCHY BOMBAY STREET SALAD CUPS

This crunchy salad is inspired by the Mumbai Indian street food snack (chaat) bhel puri.

- **125g (4oz) cherry tomatoes**
- **½ lebanese cucumber (65g)**
- **½ shallot**
- **¼ cup (70g) coconut yoghurt**
- **1 tablespoon mango chutney**
- **½ teaspoon curry powder**
- **½ cup (95g) drained canned chickpeas (garbanzo beans)**
- **2 tablespoons finely chopped fresh coriander (cilantro)**
- **¼ cup (6g) puffed brown rice**
- **2 tablespoons roasted unsalted peanuts**
- **1 tablespoon dried sweetened cranberries**
- **1 wedge lime**
- **2 mini paddadums (5g), to serve (optional)**

1 Cut cherry tomatoes in half. Thinly slice cucumber into matchsticks. Finely chop shallot; you will need 2 teaspoons.

2 Spoon yoghurt and chutney into a 2 cup (500ml) jar with a lid (or small takeaway bowl with lid) and sprinkle over curry powder.

3 Layer chickpeas, tomato, cucumber, shallot and coriander on yoghurt mixture in the jar. Season with salt and pepper. Top with puffed rice, peanuts and cranberries (the puffed rice needs to go on top of the vegetables so it doesn't go soggy).

4 To serve, squeeze juice from lime over salad. Replace lid and shake (or toss salad in bowl). Serve with pappadums for scooping.

tip Place 2 pappadums directly onto a microwave turntable (on opposite sides) and cook on HIGH (100%) for 45 seconds or until puffed and crisp.

food swap If you prefer, you can use chopped mint instead of coriander.

Office detox

PEPPERMINT PICK-ME UP

PREP TIME 5 MINUTES **SERVES** 1

Place ½ cup loosely packed fresh mint leaves, 1 teaspoon cacoa nibs, 1 teaspoon coconut nectar syrup or pure maple syrup into a heatproof mug. Add 1 cup (250ml) boiling water; stand for at least 5 minutes.

tips Peppermint is associated with alertness and can aid with sluggish digestion. Cacoa nibs, also assist in providing an extra pick-me-up and can be nibbled on once you've finished.

FRUITY HIBISCUS TEA SODA

PREP TIME 5 MINUTES (+ COOLING & REFRIGERATION)
MAKES 2 CUPS CONCENTRATE

Place 1 tablespoon hibiscus tea into a heatproof jug with 1 teaspoon vanilla bean paste. Pour in 2 cups (500ml) boiling water; leave to cool. Strain and chill tea concentrate. To use, combine 1 cup concentrate to 1 litre (4 cups) mineral water.

tip Hibiscus tea has a sweet tang, while vanilla has the ability to make things taste sweeter.

Did you know that most likely you will spend 18 years of your life in an office? Work smarts should include good hydration for mental alertness and to assist in recognising genuine hunger.

WATER WITH A TWIST

PREP TIME 5 MINUTES **MAKES** 1 LITRE

Choose one or two of the following:

- **½ lebanese cucumber (65g), peeled into ribbons**
- **6 mint or basil leaves**
- **10 blueberries + a wedge of lemon or orange**
- **¼ nectarine or plum**

Place fruit into a 1 litre (4-cup) drink bottle and crush down using the end of a wooden spoon. If using cucumber, place into the bottle. For herbs, crush lightly before adding. Fill the bottle with water; seal and chill.

CHOCOLATE MYLK

PREP TIME 10 MINUTES **MAKES** 1 LITRE (4 CUPS)

Blend 1 cup natural almonds, 1 litre (4 cups) water and ¼ cup cacao with 4 pitted fresh dates and ¼ cup pure maple syrup (or stevia, to taste) for 1 minute or until as smooth as possible. Strain mixture through a sieve lined with muslin (or use a nut bag), wring to extract as much liquid as possible. Pour into a 1 litre (4 cup) bottle or smaller bottles and refrigerate for up to 3 days. Shake well before using.

PREP + COOK TIME 1 HOUR MAKES 18 PIECES

VEGAN BENTO BOX

You will need a sushi mat to roll the sushi; found in the cookware aisle of major supermarkets.

- **1 cup (200g) sushi rice**
- **2 tablespoons sushi seasoning**
- **2 large roma (egg) tomatoes (160g)**
- **2 tablespoons soy sauce**
- **5g (¼oz) dried wakame seaweed, ground (see tip)**
- **2 teaspoons grated fresh ginger**
- **2 teaspoons sriracha**
- **1 teaspoon sesame oil**
- **3 sheets nori (10g)**
- **½ small avocado (100g), cut into cubes**
- **½ small lebanese cucumber (50g), cut into 1cm (½in) batons**
- **80g (2½oz) frozen shelled edamame (soybeans), blanched**
- **2 tablespoons pickled pink ginger**
- **1 teaspoon sesame seeds, toasted**
- **1 tablespoon vegan mayonnaise (just like mayo, see page 17)**

1 Place rice in sieve, rinse under cold running water until water runs clear. Place rinsed rice in a saucepan with 1½ cups (375ml) water; bring to the boil. Reduce heat to low; cook, covered, for 10 minutes or until water is absorbed. Remove pan from heat; stand, covered, for 5 minutes. While rice is still hot, add sushi seasoning; stir with a fork for 5 minutes or until sticky and slightly cooled.

2 Score a cross into the base of each tomato; place in a heatproof bowl. Pour over boiling water to cover; stand for 1 minute or until skins start to peel away. Using a slotted spoon, transfer tomatoes to a bowl of iced water. When cool enough to handle, peel away skins.

3 Cut tomatoes in half through the middle, scoop out seeds and discard. Cut flesh into 1cm (½in) dice.

4 Whisk soy sauce, ground seaweed, ginger, sriracha and sesame oil in a small bowl until combined. Add diced tomato; stir to coat. Stand 30 minutes.

5 Place nori sheet, shiny-side down, onto a sushi mat with the long side in front of you. Using damp hands, spread 1 cup rice over nori leaving a 2cm (¾in) strip at the top. Place one third of the tomato mixture, avocado and cucumber across the centre of the rice. Using sushi mat, roll up firmly away from you. Dampen nori strip lightly and seal. Repeat twice more with remaining ingredients to make three sushi rolls.

6 Cut each sushi roll into six pieces. Serve sushi with edamame, pickled ginger, sesame seeds and vegan mayonnaise.

tip Use a spice grinder or high powered mini food processor to grind seaweed to a coarse powder.

PREP + COOK TIME 20 MINUTES **SERVES** 2

TAMARI NOODLE SALAD JARS

If you don't have kimchi, toss the cabbage in 1 teaspoon rice wine vinegar before layering.

- 100g (3oz) dried rice stick noodles
- 250g (8oz) firm tofu, cubed
- 1 cup (80g) finely shredded red cabbage
- 2 small carrot (140g), julienned or grated
- 2 tablespoons kimchi
- 1 cup (80g) bean sprouts
- ½ cup fresh coriander (cilantro) leaves
- ½ cup fresh mint leaves

SESAME DRESSING

- 6cm (2½in) fresh ginger
- 2 tablespoons tamari
- 1 tablespoon sesame oil
- 1 tablespoon extra virgin olive oil
- 1 tablespoon rice wine vinegar

1 Cook noodles in a medium saucepan of boiling water for 6 minutes or until tender. Drain; rinse under running cold water.

2 Make sesame dressing.

3 Place tofu cubes into two 3½ cup (875ml) jars with a lid; pour dressing over tofu. Layer with the cabbage, carrot, noodles, kimchi and bean sprouts, then top with herbs. Cover jars with the lid. Refrigerate until ready to eat.

4 To serve, pour contents into a bowl and toss to combine.

sesame dressing Peel and finely grate ginger. Squeeze grated ginger in your hand over a small bowl to extract juice; you should have approximately 1 teaspoon ginger juice. Discard ginger pulp. Add remaining ingredients to bowl; mix to combine.

LAZY VEGAN

PREP + COOK TIME 15 MINUTES **MAKES** 2

TOFU BANH MI ROLLS

Banh mi are Vietnamese filled baguettes. Try to find bread rolls that are crusty like a baguette.

- **150g (4½oz) coleslaw salad mix**
- **¼ cup fresh coriander (cilantro)**
- **¼ cup (75g) vegan mayonnaise (just like mayo, see page 17)**
- **2 teaspoons rice wine vinegar**
- **½ teaspoon sesame oil**
- **½ teaspoon sea salt flakes**
- **1 teaspoon olive oil**
- **200g (6½oz) satay marinated tofu (see vegan hack)**
- **2 long white crusty bread rolls (140g)**

1 Place coleslaw salad mix and coriander in a medium bowl. Add 1 tablespoon of the vegan mayonnaise, the rice wine vinegar, sesame oil and salt; toss to coat well.

2 Heat oil in a medium frying pan medium-high heat; cook marinated tofu, for 2 minutes on each side, or until golden and heated through.

3 Split bread rolls in half; spread both sides with remaining mayonnaise. Fill with tofu and coleslaw mixture.

food swap Use your favourite Asian-style marinated tofu instead of the satay.

vegan hack To make your own satay marinated tofu, combine 2 tablespoons crunchy peanut butter, 1 tablespoon kecap manis and 2 teaspoons peanut oil with 200g (6½oz) firm tofu; refrigerate for 20 minutes before cooking.

PREP + COOK TIME 20 MINUTES **SERVES** 2

MUSHROOM, SPINACH & WALNUT PASTA

Packs of asian mixed mushrooms include king brown, enoki, shiitake, oyster and shimiji.

- **⅓ cup (80ml) extra virgin olive oil**
- **½ cup (50g) walnuts**
- **125g (4oz) spelt spirals (see tip)**
- **150g (4½oz) asian mixed mushrooms, sliced**
- **2 cloves garlic, chopped finely**
- **1 fresh long red chilli, seeded, chopped finely**
- **2 teaspoons apple cider vinegar**
- **280g (9oz) baby spinach leaves, washed**

1 Heat 1 tablespoon olive oil in a small frying pan over medium heat; cook walnuts, stirring continuously, for 5 minutes or until golden and toasted. Remove from pan; cool. Chop nuts coarsely.

2 Cook pasta in a large saucepan of boiling salted water for 12 minutes or until almost tender. Drain. Return pasta to pan off the heat; cover and keep warm.

3 Heat remaining olive oil in a medium saucepan over medium-high heat; cook mushrooms for 2 minutes or until tender and golden. Add garlic and chilli; cook stirring, for 1 minute or until fragrant. Add vinegar; cook for 1 minute. Add spinach and toasted walnuts; cook for 1 minute or until spinach is lightly wilted. Season.

4 Add mushroom mixture to pasta; toss well to coat pasta. Serve.

tip You can use any shaped spelt pasta for this recipe.

vegan hack Spelt is an ancient grain with similarities to wheat. Unlike plain flour, which is refined by removing the germ and the bran, the nutritious part of the spelt grain remains when it's milled into wholemeal flour.

PREP + COOK TIME 15 MINUTES SERVES 2

SPICY BEAN QUESADILLAS

It is worth adding a Mexican-style hot sauce to your condiment arsenal to pep-up endless recipes.

- 4 flour tortillas (160g)
- ¾ cup (180g) refried black beans (see food swaps)
- 100g (3oz) firm tofu, chopped finely
- 100g (3oz) chopped drained roasted red capsicums (bell peppers)
- 1 small zucchini (90g), peeled into ribbons
- 2 tablespoons pickled jalapeños
- olive oil cooking spray
- 1 medium avocado (250g), sliced
- mexican hot sauce, coriander leaves and lime wedges, to serve

1 Place tortillas on a work bench; spread with refried beans. Top two tortillas with tofu, capsicum, zucchini and jalapeños. Top with remaining tortillas, bean-side down; press to seal slightly.

2 Heat a large frying pan or grill plate over medium-high heat; spray with oil. Cook quesadillas, one at a time, for 2 minutes each side or until golden and crisp. (Alternatively, toast in a baking-paper-lined sandwich press for 4 minutes.)

3 Cut quesadillas into wedges; top with avocado. Serve with hot sauce, coriander and lime wedges.

food swaps You can use refried kidney beans instead the black beans if they are not available or simply to try a different flavour.

PREP + COOK TIME 20 MINUTES **SERVES** 4

LOADED SWEET POTATOES WITH CHICKPEA TABBOULEH

Try to buy sweet potatoes that are equal in length and width so that they cook evenly in the microwave.

- **4 small orange sweet potatoes (1kg)**
- **400g (12½oz) can chickpeas (garbanzo beans), drained, rinsed, chopped coarsely**
- **2 small tomatoes (180g), chopped finely**
- **1 lebanese cucumber (130g), chopped finely**
- **2 green onions (scallion), chopped finely**
- **½ cup small mint leaves (see tip)**
- **½ cup (130g) hummus**
- **2 tablespoons lemon juice**
- **2 tablespoons water**
- **1 tablespoon extra virgin olive oil**
- **¼ teaspoon sumac**

1 Pierce sweet potatoes a few times with a sharp knife. Microwave on HIGH (100%) for 8 minutes or until soft.

2 Meanwhile, combine chickpeas, tomato, cucumber, green onion and mint in a medium bowl; season.

3 Whisk hummus, lemon juice and the water in a small bowl until smooth; season to taste.

4 Cut sweet potatoes lengthways along the top, being careful not to cut all the way through. Squeeze the sides gently to create a well in the centre. Fill potatoes with chickpea tabbouleh; drizzle with hummus dressing and olive oil then sprinkle with sumac.

tip We used small mint leaves in this recipe, you can use any other soft herbs such as flat-leaf parsley or coriander (cilantro). If the leaves are large, coarsely chop them.

food swaps You can use kidney or black beans instead of chickpeas.

PREP + COOK TIME 20 MINUTES **SERVES** 2

MIXED GRAIN BOWL

There are an assortment of grain and pulse mixes available these days; experiment with other types.

- ⅓ cup (80ml) extra virgin olive oil
- 1 clove garlic, crushed
- 250g (8oz) packet microwave brown rice and quinoa
- 300g (9½oz) brussels sprouts, trimmed, halved
- 150g (4½oz) cavolo nero (tuscan kale), trimmed
- 1 medium avocado (250g), sliced
- ¼ cup (50g) pepitas (pumpkin seed kernels), toasted
- 1 tablespoon fresh basil leaves

TAHINI DRESSING

- 2 tablespoons tahini
- ¼ cup fresh basil leaves
- 3 teaspoons white wine vinegar
- ½ cup (125ml) water

1 Make tahini dressing.

2 Heat 2 tablespoons of the oil in a large frying pan over medium-high heat. Add garlic; cook for 30 seconds. Add rice and quinoa mix; cook, stirring, for 5 minutes or until starting to crisp. Transfer rice mixture to a bowl; cover to keep warm.

3 Heat 1 tablespoon of the oil in same pan; cook brussels sprouts, turning occasionally, for 5 minutes or until charred and tender. Transfer to a plate; cover to keep warm.

4 Heat remaining oil in same pan; cook cavolo nero, turning, for 2 minutes or until just starting to wilt. Transfer to plate; cover to keep warm.

5 Divide rice mixture between bowls; top with brussels sprouts, cavolo nero, avocado and pepitas. Drizzle with dressing and top with basil leaves.

tahini dressing Process ingredients in a small food processor until smooth. Season to taste.

PREP + COOK TIME 30 MINUTES SERVES 2

SWEET & SPICY TOFU NOODLES

To make your own stir-fry mix, combine broccoli florets, sugar snap peas and red capsicum strips.

- **200g (6½oz) dried rice stick noodles**
- **250g (8oz) firm tofu**
- **1 tablespoon peanut oil**
- **1 clove garlic, crushed**
- **1 tablespoon finely chopped fresh ginger**
- **250g (8oz) packet fresh stir-fry vegetables**
- **¼ cup (60ml) sweet chilli sauce**
- **2 tablespoons sriracha**
- **2 teaspoons tamari**
- **50g (1½oz) bean sprouts, plus extra to serve**
- **2 tablespoons fried shallots**
- **⅓ cup loosely packed fresh coriander (cilantro) leaves**

1 Place noodles in a large heatproof bowl; pour in enough boiling water to cover. Stand for 5 minutes or until noodles soften. Drain.

2 Meanwhile, pat tofu dry with paper towel to remove as much moisture as possible. Cut tofu into 2cm (¾in) cubes.

3 Heat oil in a wok or large frying pan over medium-high heat. Add tofu; cook for 1 minute each side or until golden. Remove with a slotted spoon. Add garlic, ginger and stir-fry vegetables to wok; cook for 1 minute or until vegetables are just starting to soften.

4 Add noodles, combined sauces and bean sprouts; stir-fry gently to prevent noodles breaking up, or until combined and heated through.

5 Divide mixture between bowls. Top with tofu, extra bean sprouts, fried shallots and coriander.

food swap You could also serve the stir-fry topped with sliced chilli, chopped peanuts and lime wedges.

PREP + COOK TIME 35 MINUTES **MAKES** 12

CHILLI LARB LETTUCE CUPS

Tempeh, fermented tofu, replaces meat in this traditional Lao and northeast Thai banquet dish.

- 250g (8oz) tempeh
- 1 tablespoon sesame oil
- 1½ tablespoons peanut oil
- 1 clove garlic, crushed
- 1 tablespoon grated fresh ginger
- 2 tablespoons soy sauce
- ¼ cup (35g) coarsely chopped peanuts
- ½ teaspoon chilli flakes
- 12 cos (romaine) lettuce leaves (180g)
- ¼ cup fresh coriander (cilantro) leaves
- lime wedges, to serve

QUICK PICKLE

- 1 lebanese cucumber (130g)
- 1 small red onion (100g)
- 1 fresh long red chilli
- ½ cup (125ml) apple cider vinegar
- 1½ teaspoons palm sugar (see food swap)

1 Make quick pickle.

2 Pat tempeh dry with paper towel; crumble using your hands.

3 Heat sesame oil and 1 tablespoon of the peanut oil in a frying pan over medium-high heat. Add crumbled tempeh; cook, stirring, for 6 minutes breaking up any clumps or until starting to crisp slightly. Add garlic and ginger; cook for 1 minute or until fragrant. Add 1½ tablespoons of the soy sauce; cook, stirring for a further 2 minutes or until coated. Transfer to a bowl; keep warm.

4 Return pan to medium-high heat, add remaining peanut oil and chopped peanuts; cook, tossing, for 1½ minutes or until peanuts are lightly toasted. Add remaining soy sauce and the chilli flakes; cook, tossing, for a further 1 minute to coat. Remove from heat.

5 Fill lettuce leaves with tempeh mixture; top with quick pickle, soy-coated peanuts and coriander. Serve with lime wedges.

quick pickle Cut cucumber in half lengthways, remove seeds; slice thinly. Thinly slice onion and chilli crossways. Place onion and chilli in a small bowl and cucumber in a second small bowl. Divide vinegar and sugar between bowls; season each mixture with a pinch of salt, then toss to coat. Stand for at least 15 minutes to pickle. Drain and combine before using.

food swap You can use brown sugar or coconut sugar instead of the palm sugar. You could also use caster (superfine) sugar.

PREP + COOK TIME 45 MINUTES **SERVES** 2

SUNFLOWER SEED BOLOGNESE

Sunflower seeds are a good vegan source of valuable nutrients such as protein and iron!

- 100g (3oz) sunflower seeds
- 1½ cups (375ml) boiling water
- 2 tablespoons extra virgin olive oil
- ½ medium onion (75g), chopped finely
- 1 small carrot (70g), chopped finely
- 2 cloves garlic, crushed
- 1 tablespoon fresh thyme leaves, chopped
- 2 teaspoons finely chopped fresh rosemary leaves
- ¼ cup (70g) tomato paste
- 400g (12½oz) can cherry tomatoes
- ½ teaspoon smoked paprika
- 200g (6½oz) egg-free pappardelle (see vegan hacks)
- vegan parmesan (see page 17) and fresh basil leaves, to serve

1 Process sunflower seeds in a small food processor until very finely chopped. Transfer seeds to a heatproof bowl; pour over the boiling water. Soak for 15 minutes.

2 Meanwhile, heat oil in a medium saucepan over medium heat. Add onion and carrot; cook for 4 minutes or until softened. Add garlic and herbs; cook for a further 2 minutes or until fragrant. Add sunflower seeds and the soaking liquid to the pan, along with tomato paste, canned tomatoes and paprika. Bring to a simmer; cook for 10 minutes or until thickened. Season to taste.

3 Meanwhile, bring a large saucepan of salted water to the boil over high heat. Cook pasta for 10 minutes or until just tender; drain.

4 Toss pasta through the sauce. Serve in bowls, topped with parmesan and basil.

vegan hacks Pasta is either made from durum wheat and water or may also have the addition of egg, especially for noodles and pappadelle; check the packet to ensure the pasta is free from animal products. You can also use fresh lasagne sheets, cut into long strips or spaghetti.

PREP + COOK TIME 20 MINUTES **SERVES** 2

POLENTA WITH RAINBOW CHARD & CHILLI BEANS

Rainbow chard is silver beet with brightly coloured yellow, orange and red stalks.

- **1 bunch rainbow chard (750g), trimmed (see food swap)**
- **2 vegan vegetable stock cubes**
- **¼ cup (60ml) extra virgin olive oil**
- **2 cloves garlic, sliced**
- **400g (12½oz) can cannellini beans, drained, rinsed**
- **¾ teaspoon dried chilli flakes**
- **¾ cup (130g) instant polenta (cornmeal)**
- **½ medium lemon (70g), cut into wedges**

1 Tear leaves from chard stalks. Using a vegetable peeler, peel stalks into thin ribbons. Place ribbons in a bowl of iced water for 5 minutes or until curled.

2 Place 1 litre (4 cups) water in a medium saucepan with crumbled stock cubes; bring to a simmer over medium-high heat.

3 Meanwhile, heat 2 tablespoons of the olive oil in a large frying pan over medium-high heat. Add garlic; cook for a few minutes or until golden. Remove with a slotted spoon; reserve for serving. Add beans and chilli flakes to pan; cook, stirring, for 5 minutes or until bean skins are crisp. Remove with a slotted spoon.

4 Heat remaining oil in same pan; cook chard stems, stirring for 3 minutes or until tender and crisp. Add chard leaves and 2 tablespoons water; cook, covered, for 2 minutes or until leaves just wilt. Season to taste.

5 Slowly add polenta to simmering stock in a thin steady stream, whisking continuously. Reduce heat to low-medium; continue whisking for 2 minutes or until polenta boils and thickens. Remove from heat; stir with a wooden spoon for 1 minute. Season to taste.

6 Ladle soft polenta over a platter, top with a pile of chard mixture and crisp beans; sprinkle with fried garlic. Drizzle with a little extra olive oil, if you like. Serve immediately (polenta will thicken on standing), with lemon wedges.

vegan hack To increase the bio-availability of the iron in the chard leaves serve with lemon wedges.

food swap You can use regular silver beet instead of rainbow chard.

PREP + COOK TIME 30 MINUTES SERVES 2

CAULI STEAKS WITH ALMONDS & TAHINI

Loose ready-to-use pomegranate seeds (arils) can be found in the fresh food section of supermarkets.

- 1 medium cauliflower (1.5kg)
- ¼ cup (60ml) extra virgin olive oil
- 2 teaspoons cumin seeds
- ⅓ cup (30g) natural sliced almonds
- 2 tablespoons tahini
- 2 tablespoons lemon juice
- 2 tablespoons pomegranate seeds (see tip)
- 2 tablespoons mint leaves

1 Preheat oven to 200°C/400°F.

2 Cut cauliflower into four 2cm (¾in) thick slices, leaving base and outer leaves intact. Place cauliflower steaks and any off-cuts, on an oiled oven tray. Brush with 2 tablespoons of the olive oil and sprinkle with the cumin seeds.

3 Bake cauliflower for 20 minutes or until golden and tender. Turn steaks over, scatter with almonds; bake for a further 5 minutes or until tender.

4 Meanwhile, combine tahini, lemon juice, remaining olive oil and 2 tablespoons water until well combined. Season.

5 Place cauli steaks on a platter, drizzle with tahini sauce. Top with pomegranate seeds and mint leaves.

tip To remove the seeds from a fresh pomegranate, cut in half crossways. Hold the cut half, cut-side down over a bowl and hit the side of the pomegranate with a wooden spoon until all the seeds fall out.

food swap You can use raisins or chopped dried figs instead of pomegranate seeds.

serving ideas Sprinkle with grated lemon rind and serve with lemon wedges.

Real-minute noodles

TOFU TOM YUM

PREP + COOK TIME 5 MINUTES **SERVES** 1

Place 1 teaspoon vegetarian tom yum paste in a 2-cup (500ml) heatproof jar with a fitted lid. Add 20g (1oz) dried rice vermicelli noodles, 3 halved cherry tomatoes, 60g (2oz) diced tofu, 2 torn oyster mushrooms, 1 tablespoon ginger cut into matchsticks, 1 torn fresh kaffir lime leaf, 1 tablespoon bean sprouts and coriander (cilantro) leaves. To serve, pour in 1½ cups boiling water, stir to combine. Cover with the lid; stand for 3 minutes. Serve with a lime wedge.

GREEN CURRY NOODLES

PREP + COOK TIME 5 MINUTES **SERVES** 1

Stir together 1½ tablespoons bottled vegan green curry paste and ¼ cup coconut cream in a 2-cup (500ml) heatproof jar with a fitted lid. Top with 10g (½oz) brown (or white) rice vermicelli noodles, ¼ cup small broccoli florets, 2 tablespoons frozen peas, ¼ cup baby spinach leaves and 1 thinly sliced green onion (scallion). To serve, pour in 1½ cups boiling water; stir to combine. Cover with the lid; stand for 3 minutes.

THAI CURRY LAKSA

PREP + COOK TIME 5 MINUTES **SERVES** 1

Stir together 1½ tablespoons bottled vegan red curry paste and ¼ cup coconut cream in a 2-cup (500ml) heatproof jar with a fitted lid. Top with ½ cup coarsely shredded asian greens, ¼ cup snow peas, 20g (¾oz) fresh thin rice noodles and ¼ cup tofu puffs. To serve, pour in 1½ cups boiling water; stir to combine. Cover with the lid; stand for 3 minutes. Serve topped with 1 tablespoon each fried shallots and thai basil leaves.

MISO RAMEN NOODLES

PREP + COOK TIME 5 MINUTES **SERVES** 1

Stir together 2 teaspoons white (shiro) miso, 1 teaspoon sesame oil and 1 teaspoon grated ginger in a 2-cup (500ml) heatproof jar with a fitted lid. Top with 50g (1½oz) cubed silken tofu, ¼ small (17g) carrot cut into julienne (matchsticks), 90g (3oz) ramen noodles, ¼ cup shelled thawed edamame (soybeans) and 25g (¾oz) enoki mushrooms. To serve, pour in 1½ cups boiling water; stir to combine. Cover with the lid; stand for 3 minutes. Serve topped with 1 green onion (scallion) sliced on the diagonal.

PREP + COOK TIME 1 HOUR 20 MINUTES **SERVES** 4

COCONUT & SPLIT PEA CURRY

Keep it simple if you like or serve topped with coriander and mint leaves, and a wedge of lime.

- **1 cup (200g) yellow split peas**
- **600g (1¼lb) jap pumpkin, peeled, seeded, cut into 3cm (1¼in) cubes**
- **¼ cup (60ml) olive oil**
- **1 large onion (200g), diced**
- **1 teaspoons finely grated ginger**
- **4 cloves garlic, crushed**
- **1 tablespoon garam masala**
- **1 litre (4 cups) vegetable stock**
- **270ml can coconut cream**
- **250g (8oz) green beans, trimmed**
- **1 tablespoon fresh lime juice**
- **coriander (cilantro) leaves, mint leaves, nigella seeds and lime wedges, to serve**

1 Place split peas in a large heatproof bowl with enough boiling water to cover. Stand until required.

2 Preheat oven to 220°C/425°F. Oil and line a large oven tray.

3 Place pumpkin on tray; drizzle with a little of the oil. Season to taste. Roast for 25 minutes or until golden.

4 Heat remaining oil in a large saucepan over medium heat. Cook onion for 4 minutes or until softened. Add ginger and garlic; cook for 1 minute. Stir in garam masala; cook for a further minute or until fragrant.

5 Add drained split peas and stock to the saucepan. Increase heat to high; cook, stirring frequently, for 30 minutes or until split peas are soft and curry is thick.

6 Reduce heat to medium, add coconut cream, green beans and roasted pumpkin; stir to combine. Simmer for 2 minutes or until beans are just tender. Stir through lime juice, season to taste. Serve curry topped with herbs, nigella seeds and lime wedges.

vegan hacks Split peas are a nutrient-dense legume containing: fibre, iron, protein, minerals and vitamins A and B to support a good immune system, eyesight, assist red blood cell production and help convert energy from the foods we eat.

serving idea Serve with brown rice.

PREP + COOK TIME 20 MINUTES **MAKES** 2

MUSHROOM 'STEAK' SANDWICH

This lazy recipe is also easy on the hip pocket with only a few fresh ingredients needed.

- **¼ cup (60ml) olive oil**
- **1 large onion (200g), sliced thinly**
- **1 large green capsicum (bell pepper) (350g), sliced thinly**
- **375g (12oz) portobello mushrooms, sliced**
- **2 cloves garlic, crushed**
- **2 tablespoons smokey barbecue sauce**
- **⅓ cup (80ml) vegan beef-like stock (see tip)**
- **2 slices vegan cheddar (36g), halved**
- **2 long seeded bread rolls (100g), split in half**
- **2 tablespoons american mustard**
- **fresh or pickled sliced jalapeño chillies, to serve (optional)**

1 Heat olive oil in a large non-stick frying pan over high heat; cook onion and capsicum for 4 minutes or until softened. Add mushrooms; cook stirring, for 5 minutes or until golden. Add garlic; stir for 1 minute. Add barbecue sauce and stock; cook for 2 minutes or until thickened. Season to taste.

2 Place vegan cheddar in rolls, spoon hot mushroom mixture on top. Drizzle with mustard; top with sliced jalapeño chillies.

tip There are an assortment of vegan stocks in the market place that mimic chicken and beef flavours, these are labelled beef or chicken 'like' and contain no animal products.

vegan hack Mushrooms have a savoury umami quality and a dense texture much like meat. They have a low calorific density and contain an important mix of minerals and vitamins. Mushrooms are also one of the leading plant-based sources for selenium, an antioxidant that assists in warding off chronic diseases.

PREP + COOK TIME 40 MINUTES **SERVES** 4

SUPER-GREENS VEGETABLE CURRY

Blitzing the ingredients in a food processor makes it easy to whip up your own curry paste at home.

- **4 cloves garlic**
- **1 cup fresh basil leaves**
- **¼ cup (40g) finely chopped fresh ginger**
- **1 bunch fresh coriander (cilantro), stalks and roots reserved, washed**
- **2 fresh long green chillies, seeded, sliced thinly**
- **400g (12½oz) kale, sliced**
- **½ cup (125ml) grapeseed oil**
- **2 medium eggplants (600g), cut into 4cm (1½in) rounds**
- **1 cup (200g) pearl barley, rinsed**
- **400ml can coconut milk**
- **1 cup (250ml) vegetable stock**
- **300g (9½oz) sugar snap peas, trimmed**
- **1 cup (120g) frozen peas, thawed**

1 Process garlic, basil, ginger, reserved coriander stalks and roots, and half each of the chilli, kale and oil until a smooth paste forms. Reserve ¼ cup curry paste.

2 Heat remaining oil in a large heavy-based saucepan over high heat; cook eggplant, in batches, for 3 minutes each side or until golden and soft. Drain on paper towel; keep warm.

3 Cook barley in a saucepan of simmering water for 20 minutes or until tender; drain well.

4 Reduce heat to medium, add curry paste to pan; cook, stirring, for 1 minute or until fragrant. Shake can of coconut milk well; add to pan with the stock, stir to combine well. Bring to a simmer.

5 Stir in sugar snaps and peas, remaining kale and reserved curry paste; cook for 2 minutes or until peas are just tender. Season to taste.

6 Divide barley and eggplant among plates; top with curry and scatter with coriander leaves and remaining chilli.

food swap You can use asian greens instead of the kale if you prefer.

PREP + COOK TIME 30 MINUTES SERVES 4

SMOKY SWEET CORN CHOWDER

Any leftover or unused cauliflower can be used to make cauliflower couscous on page 148.

- 3 green onions (scallions)
- ½ small cauliflower (500g), trimmed, chopped finely
- 1kg (2lb) frozen corn kernels, thawed
- 2 cups (500ml) vegetable stock
- ½ teaspoon garlic powder
- ½ teaspoon ground turmeric
- 400ml can coconut milk
- 3 cups (45g) salted natural popcorn
- 1 tablespoon smoked paprika
- 1 tablespoon extra virgin olive oil

1 Thinly slice green onions; reserve dark green tips. Place white and light green part of onions in a large saucepan with cauliflower, corn, stock, garlic powder and turmeric. Cover with a tight-fitting lid; bring to the boil. Reduce heat to medium; simmer for 20 minutes or until vegetables are tender.

2 Remove pan from heat. Using a stick blender; blend stock and vegetables until almost smooth. Return pan to medium heat; stir in coconut milk, then bring to a simmer. Season to taste.

3 Meanwhile, place popcorn and smoked paprika in a large bowl; toss until well coated.

4 Ladle soup into bowls; top with seasoned popcorn, reserved shredded green onion tips and drizzled with olive oil.

tips To finely chop cauliflower you can pulse it a few times in food processor. To thaw corn quickly, place in a colander and pour over boiling water. If you don't have a stick blender; cool the mixture slightly, then process or blend in batches.

Genius cobblers

PEACH & CINNAMON COBBLER

PREP + COOK TIME 1 HOUR **SERVES** 6

Preheat oven to 220°C/425°F. Line a 25cm (10in) skillet (base measurement) with baking paper. Cut 6 large (1.3kg) peaches in half; remove stones. Cut each half into three wedges. Place three-quarters of the peaches over the base of the pan. Sprinkle evenly with a 340g (11oz) packet vegan vanilla cake mix, top evenly with 125g (4oz) vegan margarine; sprinkle with 1 teaspoon ground cinnamon. Top with remaining peach wedges; sprinkle with 2 tablespoons brown sugar. Cover skillet with foil. Bake on the bottom shelf of the oven for 20 minutes. Remove foil; bake for a further 30 minutes or until cake mixture is browned and the centre is firm. Dust with icing (confectioners') sugar.

GINGER & PEAR COBBLER

PREP + COOK TIME 1 HOUR **SERVES** 6

Preheat oven to 220°C/425°F. Line a 17cm x 30cm (6¾in x 12in) baking dish with baking paper. Cut 6 medium (1.4kg) pears in half; remove cores. Cut each half into three wedges. Place three-quarters of the pears over the base of the dish. Sprinkle evenly with a 340g (11oz) packet vegan vanilla cake mix, top evenly with 125g (4oz) vegan margarine; scatter with 1 tablespoon shredded ginger and 2 tablespoons chopped natural almonds. Top with remaining pear wedges. Cover dish with foil. Bake on the bottom shelf of the oven for 20 minutes. Remove foil; bake for a further 20 minutes or until cake mixture is browned and the centre is firm. Drizzle with pure maple syrup.

Many home brand cake mixes are vegan. Check the ingredients listed on the packet to ensure that there are no dairy products. The cake mix is used dry; so you won't need the ingredients listed on the packet.

BLACKBERRY & APPLE COBBLER

PREP + COOK TIME 1 HOUR **SERVES** 6

Preheat oven to 220°C/425°F. Line a 26cm (10½in) skillet (base measurement) with baking paper. Cut 4 medium (600g) apples in half; remove cores. Cut each half into three wedges. Place three-quarters of the apple over the base of the skillet; top with 200g (6½oz) blackberries. Sprinkle evenly with a 340g (11oz) packet vegan vanilla cake mix, top evenly with 125g (4oz) vegan margarine evenly; sprinkle with 1 teaspoon ground cinnamon. Top with remaining apple wedges. Cover skillet with foil. Bake on the bottom shelf of the oven for 20 minutes. Remove foil; bake for a further 30 minutes or until cake mixture is browned and the centre is firm. Sprinkle with demerara sugar.

CHOCOLATE & BANANA COBBLER

PREP + COOK TIME 1 HOUR **SERVES** 6

Preheat oven to 220°C/425°F. Line a 17cm x 30cm (6¾in x 12in) baking dish with baking paper. Cut 6 small (780g) bananas in half lengthways. Place bananas, cut-side up, on the base of the dish. Sprinkle evenly with a 340g (11oz) packet vegan chocolate cake mix, top evenly with 125g (4oz) vegan margarine. Drizzle with 2 tablespoons dark rum combined with 2 tablespoons water. Top with 2 tablespoons roasted walnuts. Cover dish with foil. Bake on the bottom shelf of the oven for 20 minutes. Remove foil; bake for a further 20 minutes or until cake mixture is browned and the centre is firm. Dust with cocoa powder. Serve with vegan ice-cream, drizzled with melted vegan dark chocolate.

PREP + COOK TIME 15 MINUTES **SERVES** 4

BEETROOT & PISTACHIO CRUMBLE SUBS

Nuts equal protein, so if you don't have pistachios, scatter with almonds, walnuts, hazelnuts or pepitas.

- **1 small baguette (300g)**
- **½ cup (150g) vegan mayonnaise (just like mayo, see page 17)**
- **1½ teaspoons bottled grated horseradish**
- **⅓ cup (45g) pistachios, chopped**
- **2 tablespoons fresh thyme leaves**
- **1 tablespoon chopped fresh chives**
- **1 teaspoon finely grated lemon rind**
- **250g (8oz) vacuum-packed cooked beetroot (beets), cut into rounds**
- **2 teaspoons balsamic glaze**
- **1 small lemon (65g), cut into cheeks**
- **micro herbs, to serve (optional)**

1 Preheat a chargrill pan (or grill/broiler) to high. Split baguette in half horizontally, then cut each half into 10cm (4in) lengths. Chargrill bread pieces for 2 minutes on each side or until grill marks appear.

2 Combine mayonnaise and horseradish in a small bowl; season to taste.

3 Combine pistachios, thyme, chives and lemon rind in a small bowl. Season well.

4 Spread mayonnaise mixture over baguette halves. Top with beetroot slices and pistachio mixture. Drizzle with balsamic glaze and serve with lemon cheeks.

tip Vacuum-packed cooked beetroot is available in the fresh food section in most large supermarkets.

FAST FOOD

PREP + COOK TIME 25 MINUTES (+ COOLING) **MAKES** 10

VEGETABLE SPRING ROLLS

A good spring roll has a crisp exterior with an abundant flavoursome filling. These won't disappoint!

- **50g (1½oz) dried rice vermicelli noodles**
- **1 tablespoon peanut oil**
- **1 clove garlic, crushed**
- **2 tablespoons finely chopped fresh ginger**
- **1 shallot, sliced thinly**
- **1 large carrot (180g), cut into matchsticks**
- **½ teaspoon chinese five spice**
- **2 cups (160g) shredded wombok (napa cabbage)**
- **1 teaspoon sesame oil**
- **2 tablespoons tamari**
- **1 teaspoon cornflour (cornstarch)**
- **10 x 20cm (8in) frozen spring roll wrappers (see tip)**
- **3 cups (750ml) vegetable oil**

1 Place vermicelli in a medium bowl of boiling water for 2 minutes or until soft. Drain well. Using scissors, snip noodles into shorter length.

2 Heat oil in a large frying pan or wok over medium-high heat. Add garlic, ginger, shallot and carrot; stir-fry for 5 minutes or until carrot is soft. Stir in five spice, wombok and sesame oil; cook for 1 minute.

3 Combine tamari and cornflour in a small bowl. Add to vegetables, stir until thickened slightly. Transfer mixture to bowl, stir in vermicelli until combined. Cool to room temperature.

4 Place a spring roll wrapper on flat surface. Place ¼ cup of filling, one-third up from the bottom edge in a line, leaving 1.5cm (¾in) border at each side. Fold over once, then fold in the sides and roll up to enclose filling; brush the join with a little water to seal. Repeat with remaining wrappers and filling.

5 Heat oil in a medium saucepan over medium heat until 190°C/375°F (or until a cube of bread browns in 10 seconds). Fry spring rolls for 3 minutes or until golden and crisp. Drain on paper towel over a wire rack.

tip You will find spring roll wrappers in the freezer section of the supermarket. Thaw before using.

serving idea Serve spring rolls with a sweet chilli sauce or sriracha for an extra chilli kick.

PREP + COOK TIME 30 MINUTES SERVES 4

BEER BATTERED POTATO SCALLOPS WITH MINTY EDAMAME

This fish shop favourite also goes well with our faux fish 'bliss' and tartare sauce on page 133.

- 500g (1lb) potatoes
- 250g (8oz) orange sweet potatoes
- 400g (12½oz) frozen shelled edamame (soybeans)
- ½ cup finely chopped fresh mint
- 1 clove garlic, crushed
- ⅓ cup (80ml) tahini
- ½ cup (125ml) water
- ¼ cup (60ml) lemon juice
- vegetable oil, for deep-frying
- 1 cup (150g) plain (all-purpose) flour
- 1¼ cups (310ml) lager beer
- malt vinegar and lemon wedges, to serve

1 Peel potatoes and sweet potatoes; cut into 1cm (½in) thick slices. Cook potatoes together in a saucepan of boiling water for 3 minutes. Drain well; pat dry with paper towel. Cool.

2 Meanwhile, cook edamame in a saucepan of boiling water for 5 minutes; drain well. Place edamame in a food processor with mint, garlic, tahini, water and lemon juice; process until well combined. Season to taste.

3 Fill a large saucepan one-third full with oil; heat to 180°C/350°F (or until a cube of bread turns golden in 15 seconds).

4 Whisk flour and beer in a medium bowl until smooth; season.

5 Dip potato slices in batter, allowing excess to drain off. Deep-fry, in two batches, for 5 minutes or until potato are tender, golden and crisp. Drain on paper towel. Sprinkle with salt.

6 Serve hot potato scallops with minty edamame, malt vinegar and lemon wedges.

tips Try to use potatoes and sweet potatoes that are the same diameter as one another. If you would like the consistency of the minty edamame to be a little runnier, just add more water when processing. Keep the first batch of scallops warm on an oven tray in a 180°C/350°F oven while you cook the second batch.

PREP + COOK TIME 40 MINUTES **SERVES** 4

SALT & PEPPER 'SQUID'

This genius idea uses palm heart rings, which have an uncanny resemblance to squid once battered.

- 4 x 400g (12½oz) cans hearts of palm
- 2 sheets nori (5g)
- 1½ cups (225g) tempura batter mix (see vegan hack)
- 1¼ cups (310ml) iced water
- 1 cup (150g) plain (all-purpose) flour
- 1 tablespoon sea salt flakes
- 1 tablespoon ground white pepper
- 1 tablespoon cajun seasoning
- 1 teaspoon sweet paprika
- ¼ teaspoon cayenne pepper
- peanut oil, for deep-frying

CHILLI & LIME MAYO

- ½ cup (150g) vegan mayonnaise (just like mayo, see page 17)
- 1½ tablespoons sriracha
- 1 tablespoon fresh lime juice

1 Make chilli and lime mayo.

2 Drain palm hearts; pat dry with paper towel. Cut into 2cm (¾in) discs. Using your fingers, carefully push the centre out from each heart (see tips). Break nori sheets into pieces, then grind to a powder in a spice grinder. (Alternatively, pulse in a food processor until finely chopped.)

3 To make batter, place tempura batter mix in a large bowl with the ground nori; whisk in the iced water until combined.

4 Place flour, salt, pepper, seasoning, paprika and cayenne in a large zip-top bag. Add palm heart rings; seal bag. Shake bag until rings are coated.

5 Fill a large saucepan or wok one-third full with oil and heat to 180°C/350°F (or until a cube of bread browns in 15 seconds). Working in batches, coat palm heart rings in batter, allowing excess to drain off; fry for 3 minutes until golden. Drain on a wire rack placed over a tray. Season. Serve hot with chilli and lime mayo.

chilli & lime mayo Combine ingredients in a small bowl.

tips The palm heart offcuts can be added to a salad or blended with any leftover chilli and lime mayo to make a dip. Place salt and pepper 'squid' in a 150°C/300°F oven to keep warm while you cook remaining batches.

serving ideas Serve with shoestring fries and lime wedges.

vegan hack Tempura batter mix is available from the Asian food section of major supermarkets. Check the packet label to ensure the brand is vegan.

PREP + COOK TIME 1 HOUR 5 MINUTES **MAKES** 12

SWEET POTATO, BLACK BEAN & FETTA SAUSAGE ROLLS

You can make the sausage rolls with vegan fetta as we have here or spiced tofu.

- **750g (1½lb) orange sweet potatoes, peeled, cut into 2cm (¾in) cubes**
- **1 medium red onion (170g), chopped finely**
- **olive oil cooking spray**
- **400g (12½oz) can black beans, drained, rinsed**
- **⅓ cup coarsely chopped fresh flat-leaf parsley**
- **¼ cup (40g) pine nuts, toasted, chopped coarsely**
- **100g (3oz) marinated vegan almond fetta (see tip), crumbled**
- **2 sheets frozen vegan puff pastry (330g), just thawed**
- **1 tablespoon soy milk**
- **2 teaspoons black sesame seeds**
- **2 teaspoons white sesame seeds**
- **1 cup (320g) tomato relish**

1 Preheat oven to 180°C/350°F. Line two oven trays with baking paper.

2 Place sweet potato and onion on one tray. Lightly spray with olive oil; season. Roast for 30 minutes or until sweet potato is soft. Cool slightly. Increase oven to 230°C/450°F.

3 Place roasted vegetables in a large bowl with the beans; using a fork, crush lightly. Add parsley and pine nuts; mix well. Gently fold in fetta.

4 Cut pastry sheets in half. Place a quarter of the filling mixture along one long edge; brush the opposite edge with soy milk. Roll up to enclose filling. Cut roll into three pieces; place, seam-side down, on second lined tray. Repeat with remaining pastry and filling mixture.

5 Brush top of rolls with remaining soy milk; sprinkle with combined sesame seeds.

6 Bake sausage rolls for 30 minutes or until golden brown. Serve hot or room temperature with the relish.

tip You can make the betta fetta on page 16 and use it in this recipe instead of buying it.

PREP + COOK TIME 55 MINUTES SERVES 4

BEET & BLACK BEAN BURGER

Cook up an extra batch of these patties; once cooled, freeze between freezer paper for up to 1 month.

- 2 tablespoons extra virgin olive oil
- 1 small red onion (100g), chopped finely
- 2 cloves garlic, crushed
- ¼ cup firmly packed chopped flat-leaf parsley leaves and stems
- 1 small beetroot (beets) (100g), grated coarsely
- 1 cup (125g) canned black beans
- 2 tablespoons dried breadcrumbs
- 1 tablespoon flaxseed meal
- 4 sesame seed bread rolls (360g)
- ⅓ cup (95g) tomato sauce (ketchup)
- ⅓ cup (95g) american mustard
- 2 medium tomatoes (300g), sliced
- 12 slices bread and butter pickles
- 1 cup (60g) shredded cos (romaine) lettuce

SWEET POTATO CURLY FRIES

- 1kg (2lb) orange sweet potatoes
- vegetable oil, for deep-frying

1 Heat half the olive oil in a small frying pan over medium heat; cook onion, stirring, for 3 minutes or until softened. Add garlic; cook stirring, for 1 minute or until fragrant.

2 Process onion mixture, parsley, beetroot, black beans, breadcrumbs and flaxseed meal until the mixture comes together but still retains some texture. Shape mixture into four 9cm (3¾in) patties.

3 Make sweet potato curly fries.

4 Heat remaining olive oil in a medium frying pan over medium heat. Cook patties for 3 minutes on each side or until golden and heated through. (Char patties slightly if you want a traditional chargrilled taste.)

5 Preheat grill (broiler) to high. Place rolls, cut-side up, on an oven tray. Place under grill for 5 minutes or until golden.

6 Spread tomato sauce and mustard on base of rolls; top with patties, tomato, pickles and lettuce, then roll tops. Serve burgers with curly fries.

sweet potato curly fries Using a spiraliser, cut sweet potatoes into long curly spirals. Fill a large saucepan one-third full with oil and heat to 180°C/350°F (or until a cube of bread browns in 15 seconds). Fry potato curls, in batches, for 2 minutes or until golden. Drain on a paper-towel-lined tray; season with salt.

PREP + COOK TIME 55 MINUTES (+ STANDING) **SERVES** 4

DEEP-DISH 'PEPPERONI' PIZZA

Pepperoni gets its taste from a select mix of spices; we've used the same mix to flavour these chickpeas.

- **2 teaspoons (7g) dried yeast**
- **pinch of caster (superfine) sugar**
- **½ teaspoon fine sea salt**
- **¾ cup (180ml) warm water**
- **2 cups (300g) plain (all-purpose) flour, plus extra to dust**
- **2½ tablespoons extra virgin olive oil**
- **1½ cups (420g) tomato puree**
- **180g (5½oz) vegan cheddar, grated**
- **12 fresh basil leaves**

'PEPPERONI' CHICKPEAS

- **2 tablespoons extra virgin olive oil**
- **400g (12½oz) can chickpeas (garbanzo beans), drained, rinsed**
- **1 teaspoon garlic granules (see tip)**
- **1 teaspoon fennel seeds**
- **1 teaspoon dried chilli flakes**
- **1 teaspoon onion powder**
- **1 teaspoon smoked paprika**

1 Combine yeast, sugar, salt and the warm water in a small bowl; stir until yeast dissolves. Cover; stand in a warm place for 10 minutes or until mixture is frothy.

2 Place flour in a large bowl and make a well in the centre. Add the yeast mixture and olive oil; using your hands, gradually draw the flour into the wet mixture until it forms a dough. Knead dough on a floured surface for 10 minutes or until smooth and elastic.

3 Place dough in an oiled large bowl; cover with plastic wrap. Stand in a warm place until dough has doubled in size.

4 Make 'pepperoni' chickpeas.

5 Preheat oven to 220°C/425°F. Grease a 22cm (8¾in) springform cake pan; line base with baking paper.

6 Turn dough onto a lightly floured surface; knead lightly until smooth. Roll into a 26cm (10½in) round. Line pan with dough, easing the dough into the base and part way up the side. Top with half each of the tomato puree, vegan cheddar and chickpeas. Season. Repeat layering with remaining puree, vegan cheddar and chickpeas.

7 Bake pizza for 20 minutes or until the crust is golden and cooked through. Stand pizza for 5 minutes before removing from the pan. Serve topped with basil leaves.

'pepperoni' chickpeas Heat oil in a saucepan over medium-high heat; cook chickpeas for 2 minutes. Add remaining ingredients; cook for a further 2 minutes or until fragrant. Leave to cool.

tip Garlic granules, sometimes sold as granulated garlic, are sold in small packets or jars alongside other spices in the supermarket.

Not dogs

KIMCHI NOT-DOGS

PREP + COOK TIME 20 MINUTES **SERVES** 4

In a large bowl, combine 125g (4oz) shredded white cabbage, 1 thinly sliced green onion (scallion), ⅓ cup coarsely chopped fresh coriander (cilantro), 2 tablespoons lemon juice and ¼ teaspoon sesame oil. For dressing, stir ¼ teaspoon sesame oil and ½ cup vegan mayonnaise in a small bowl; season. Heat a large, lightly oiled frying pan over high heat; cook 4 vegan hot dogs (320g) for 2 minutes. Add 1 cup (100g) chopped vegan kimchi; cook, turning, for a further 3 minutes or until warmed through. Warm 4 split long bread rolls (240g). Fill rolls with hot dogs and kimchi, then top with cabbage salad and 2 teaspoons toasted sesame seeds. Drizzle with dressing.

REUBEN NOT-DOGS

PREP + COOK TIME 30 MINUTES **SERVES** 4

For dressing, combine ¼ cup vegan mayonnaise, ½ teaspoon tamarind (or A1 steak sauce) and 1 tablespoon each tomato sauce (ketchup), sweet mustard pickle and lemon juice in a small bowl. Heat 1 tablespoon olive oil in a frying pan over low heat; cook 1 large (200g) thinly sliced onion, stirring occasionally, 15 minutes or until caramelised. Remove from pan; keep warm. Cook 4 vegan hot dogs (320g) in same pan over high heat for 5 minutes, turning, until browned. Place 4 split long bread rolls (240g) on an oven tray; top with 150g (4½oz) sliced vegan cheddar. Place under a preheated grill (broiler) for 2 minutes or until cheese melts. Fill with hot dogs, onions, ½ cup (40g) sauerkraut and ½ cup sliced dill pickles. Drizzle with dressing.

BANH MI NOT-DOGS

PREP + COOK TIME 20 MINUTES **SERVES** 4

Cut 1 small (70g) carrot and 100g (3oz) piece daikon into julienne (matchsticks); place in a medium bowl with ¼ cup rice wine vinegar, season. Stand for 10 minutes. Combine ½ cup (150g) vegan mayonnaise and 1 teaspoon sriracha in a small bowl. Heat a large, oiled frying pan over high heat; cook 4 vegan hot dogs (320g) for 5 minutes, turning, until browned. Warm 4 split long bread rolls (240g); spread with sriracha mayonnaise. Fill rolls with hot dogs. Drain carrot and daikon; place on hot dogs. Sprinkle with 1 thinly sliced green onion (scallion), ½ cup each fresh mint and coriander (cilantro) leaves and 2 tablespoons chopped roasted salted peanuts. Drizzle with extra sriracha to serve.

NACHO NOT-DOGS

PREP + COOK TIME 15 MINUTES **SERVES** 4

Preheated grill (broiler) to high. Place 4 vegan hot dogs (320g) and 1 cup (190g) mexi beans in a large, non-stick frying pan over low heat; cook, turning, for 3 minutes or until warm. Place 4 split long bread rolls (240g) rolls on an oven tray; fill rolls with 25g (¾oz) corn chips, then hot dogs and beans. Sprinkle with 1 cup grated vegan cheddar. Place under hot grill for 2 minutes or until cheese melts. Top with ⅓ cup pickled sliced jalapeño and ¼ cup chopped coriander (cilantro) leaves.

PREP + COOK TIME 35 MINUTES **MAKES** 12

TOFU CHORIZO & PICKLED PINEAPPLE SOFT TACOS

Tofu, chilli and smoked paprika are the basis for our hearty chorizo-like filling in these tacos.

- **300g (9½oz) firm tofu**
- **2 tablespoons olive oil**
- **400g (12½oz) can chickpeas (garbanzo beans), drained, rinsed**
- **1 medium red onion (170g), chopped finely**
- **1½ teaspoons smoked paprika**
- **1 teaspoon ground coriander**
- **1 teaspoon ground cumin**
- **1 clove garlic, crushed**
- **1 tablespoon finely chopped chipotle chilli in adobo sauce**
- **½ cup (125ml) water**
- **12 small white corn tortillas (300g), warmed**
- **3 cups (240g) finely shredded green cabbage**
- **1 medium avocado (250g), sliced**
- **¼ cup coarsely chopped fresh coriander (cilantro)**

PICKLED PINEAPPLE

- **½ small pineapple (450g)**
- **¼ cup (60ml) lime juice**
- **1½ tablespoons pure maple syrup**
- **1 tablespoon soy sauce**
- **4 radishes, cut into thin wedges**

1 Drain tofu; pat dry with paper towel. Crumble into pea-sized chunks.

2 Make pickled pineapple.

3 Heat olive oil in a large frying pan over medium high heat; cook chickpeas for 5 minutes or until crisp. Add tofu and onion; cook for 8 minutes or until tofu is golden and onion is lightly charred. Reduce heat to medium. Add spices and garlic; cook for 2 minutes or until fragrant. Add chilli and the water. Bring to a simmer; cook, stirring, for 2 minutes or until thickened. Season to taste.

4 To assemble, top tortillas with tofu 'chorizo' mixture, cabbage, avocado, then pickled pineapple and radishes; drizzle with a little of the pickling liquid. Top with coriander.

pickled pineapple Peel and core pineapple, then thinly slice on a mandoline, V-slicer or with a sharp knife. Stir lime juice, maple syrup and soy sauce together in a shallow dish; add pineapple slices and radishes, then toss to coat. Cover; stand for 10 minutes (or refrigerate overnight).

food swaps You can use 1 teaspoon extra smoked paprika and a little fresh chopped chilli, chilli powder or chilli flakes in place of the chipotle chilli in adobo sauce. For a gluten-free version, use tamari instead of the soy sauce.

PREP + COOK TIME 40 MINUTES SERVES 4

THAI CORN FRITTERS & GREEN PAPAYA SALAD

Use green mango, jicama (yam bean) or firm nashi pear here if green papaya are not available.

- ½ bunch fresh coriander (cilantro) with roots attached
- 500g (1lb) green papaya
- ¾ cup (135g) rice flour
- ½ teaspoon baking powder
- ⅔ cup (160ml) iced water
- 1 corn cob (250g), husk and silks removed
- 150g (4½oz) green beans, trimmed, sliced thinly
- ⅓ cup (80ml) vegetable oil
- 2 baby gem lettuce (180g), leaves separated
- 250g (8oz) cherry tomatoes, quartered

CHILLI PEANUT DRESSING

- 1 clove garlic, chopped
- 1 fresh long red chilli, chopped finely (see tip)
- ⅓ cup (45g) roasted unsalted peanuts
- ¼ cup (60ml) fresh lime juice
- 2 tablespoons coconut sugar (see food swap)
- 1 tablespoon soy sauce
- 1 tablespoon water

1 Remove roots from coriander; wash and reserve for dressing. Pick half the coriander into sprigs; reserve to serve. Finely chop remaining coriander to yield ¼ cup. Peel papaya; finely shred using a mandoline, julienne peeler or knife.

2 Make chilli peanut dressing.

3 Combine rice flour and baking powder in a large bowl. Whisk in the iced water to form a thick batter. Cut kernels from corn; add to batter with beans and chopped coriander, then mix well. Season to taste. (The mixture will look runny but binds on cooking.)

4 Heat oil in large frying pan over high heat or until a drop of batter sizzles as soon as it is added to the pan. Working in two batches of six, drop heaped tablespoons of batter into pan; cook for 3 minutes each side or until crisp and golden.

5 Place lettuce leaves and tomatoes on a large platter with corn fritters, papaya, reserved coriander sprigs and chilli peanut dressing. To eat, scoop a little bit of everything onto a lettuce leaf.

chilli peanut dressing Using a mortar and pestle, crush garlic, chilli and reserved coriander root (from step 1) with a pinch of salt to form a paste. Add peanuts; crush lightly. Stir in remaining ingredients. Spoon into a small bowl.

tip For a less spicy dressing, remove the membrane and seeds from the chilli before chopping.

food swap Use brown sugar or palm sugar instead of coconut sugar.

PREP + COOK TIME 40 MINUTES **SERVES** 4

PULLED JACKFRUIT BAO BUNS

Jackfruit is a large tropical fruit with a meaty texture and neutral taste that absorbs other flavours.

- **565g (1¼lb) can young green jackfruit in brine (see tips), drained, rinsed**
- **½ cup (130g) hoisin sauce**
- **¼ cup (60ml) water**
- **2 tablespoons pure maple syrup**
- **2 tablespoons tamari**
- **¼ teaspoon chinese five spice**
- **1 lebanese cucumber (130g), sliced thinly**
- **1 fresh long red chilli, sliced thinly**
- **2 tablespoons rice wine vinegar**
- **8 frozen mini mantou buns (180g) (see tips)**
- **2 tablespoons vegan mayonnaise (just like mayo, see page 17)**
- **1 green onion (scallion), sliced thinly**
- **⅓ cup fresh coriander (cilantro)**
- **⅓ cup (50g) roasted salted peanuts, chopped finely**

1 Cut jackfruit into 1cm (½in) slices through the core. Combine hoisin, the water, maple syrup, tamari and five spice in a medium saucepan over medium heat. Season with pepper. Add jackfruit; bring to simmer. Cook for 20 minutes, stirring and breaking jackfruit up with the back of a spoon until the sauce has thickened and the mixture resembles pulled pork.

2 Meanwhile, combine cucumber, chilli and vinegar in a medium glass or stainless steel bowl; season. Stand for 5 minutes; drain.

3 Split frozen buns three-quarters of the way through. Steam buns, covered in a bamboo steamer over a saucepan of simmering water, for 5 minutes or until puffed up and heated through.

4 Spread buns with mayonnaise; fill with jackfruit mixture, pickled cucumber mixture, green onion, coriander and peanuts.

tips Canned jackfruit can be found at Asian supermarkets. Ensure that you are buying jackfruit in brine not syrup. Mantou buns are available frozen from Asian supermarkets. You could also serve the pulled jackfruit in wraps or soft buns.

PREP + COOK TIME 1 HOUR (+ STANDING & REFRIGERATION) **SERVES** 4

BLISS & CHIPS WITH MUSHY PEAS

For all the fun of fish and chips without the fish, our battered eggplant is a delicious stand-in.

- 4 japanese eggplants (460g)
- 1 tablespoon fine sea salt
- 4 sheets nori (10g), halved
- 1¼ cups (190g) self-raising flour
- 1½ cups (375ml) pale ale
- 750g (1½lb) potatoes, scrubbed
- 2 tablespoons olive oil
- vegetable oil, for shallow-frying
- ¼ cup (35g) self-raising flour, extra
- 1 large lemon (200g), cut into cheeks

TARTARE SAUCE

- 4 cornichons
- 1 green onion (scallion)
- 1 cup (300g) vegan mayonnaise (just like mayo, see page 17)
- 2 tablespoons baby capers

MUSHY PEAS

- 2 cups (240g) frozen peas
- 50g (1½oz) vegan margarine
- 4 fresh mint sprigs
- 1 tablespoon fresh lemon juice

1 Preheat oven to 200°C/400°F. Line two oven trays with baking paper.

2 Halve eggplant lengthways; place in a colander. Sprinkle with salt; stand for 30 minutes. Rinse eggplant under cold water. Squeeze out excess water.

3 Wrap each eggplant half in a piece of nori (the moisture will help the nori stick to the eggplant). Refrigerate for 15 minutes.

4 Make tartare sauce, then the mushy peas.

5 Place flour in a bowl; season. Gradually whisk in beer to make a smooth batter. Stand batter at room temperature for 30 minutes.

6 Cut unpeeled potatoes into chunky chips. Place chips on lined oven trays; drizzle with olive oil, then season. Bake for 30 minutes or until golden and crisp.

7 Meanwhile, fill a large saucepan or deep fryer one-third full with oil; heat to 170°C/340°F (or until a cube of bread turns golden in 8 seconds). Dust eggplant in extra flour. Dip into batter, allowing excess to drain off. Fry, in two batches, for 3 minutes each, turning halfway or until golden. Drain on a paper-towel-covered wire rack.

8 Serve eggplant with chips, mushy peas, tartare sauce and lemon cheeks.

tartare sauce Finely chop cornichons and green onions. Combine with mayonnaise and capers in a small bowl.

mushy peas Cook peas, margarine, and mint in a small saucepan over medium heat for 6 minutes or until tender. Discard mint. Using a stick blender, pulse peas, leaving some whole. Season, stir in juice.

GO RAW

PREP TIME 20 MINUTES **MAKES** 12

RAW NORI ROLLS

These nori rolls are perfect for hot summer days (or nights) when all you want is a light fresh bite.

- 1 cup (150g) sunflower seeds
- 3 green onions (scallions), sliced thinly
- ¼ cup fresh coriander (cilantro) leaves
- ¼ cup (60ml) lemon juice
- 2 tablespoons tamari, plus extra to serve
- 1 clove garlic
- 6 sheets nori (15g), halved
- ¼ small red cabbage (200g), sliced finely
- 1 large carrot (180g), cut into matchsticks
- 4 baby cucumbers (120g), sliced lengthways
- ½ cup (20g) alfalfa sprouts

1 Place sunflower seeds in a medium bowl with enough cold water to cover. Stand, covered, for 4 hours. Drain, rinse under cold water; drain well.

2 Process soaked sunflower seeds with green onions, coriander, lemon juice, tamari, garlic, and ¼ cup (60ml) water until it forms a chunky paste.

3 Place a half nori sheet on a work bench. Spread one corner with 1 tablespoon of sunflower mixture, top with one-twelfth of the red cabbage, carrot, cucumber and alfalfa sprouts. Fold nori sheet over vegetables, and roll sheet away from you on a diagonal to form a cone. Dampen the edge of the nori sheet with water to seal and close. Repeat with remaining ingredients to make 12 rolls. Serve rolls with extra tamari.

PREP TIME 20 MINUTES (+ STANDING) **SERVES** 4

MISO CASHEW BOWL WITH WINTER VEG

Shiro miso is fermented faster than other types and is less salty. It has a sweeter more mellow taste.

- 1 baby fennel bulb (130g)
- 2 cups (160g) finely shredded red cabbage
- 1 medium beetroot (beet) (150g), peeled, cut into matchsticks
- 400g (12½oz) baby carrots, trimmed, peeled into ribbons
- ⅓ cup (45g) finely chopped raw cashews
- ½ cup fresh mint leaves
- sliced red chilli and lime wedges, to serve

MISO CASHEW DRESSING

- 1 cup (150g) raw cashews
- 2 tablespoons white (shiro) miso
- 2 tablespoons coconut sugar
- ½ teaspoon finely grated lime rind
- 1 fresh small red chilli, chopped
- ⅓ cup (80ml) lime juice
- ½ cup (125ml) water

1 Make miso cashew dressing.

2 Thinly slice fennel bulb and stems.

3 Divide fennel, cabbage, beetroot and carrot among bowls; top with chopped cashews and mint. Serve with dressing, chilli and lime wedges.

miso cashew dressing Place cashews in a small bowl; cover with water. Stand, covered, for 4 hours, drain. Blend soaked cashews with remaining ingredients in a high-powered blender until smooth.

tips Use a mandoline or V-slicer to cut the vegetables for best results. Toss the fennel in lime juice to prevent it from browning if not serving immediately. We used shiro miso, also known as white miso; while it is lighter than other types, it's golden in colour. Seed the chilli if you prefer less heat.

vegan hack Check the ingredients listed on the miso pastes as some brands contain bonito (tuna) extract which is unsuitable for vegans.

PREP TIME 20 MINUTES (+ OVERNIGHT REFRIGERATION) **SERVES** 4

TOMATO, AVOCADO, FIG & RAW MOZZARELLA SALAD

Cheese is often missed the most on a vegan diet, but fear-not with this fab version of mozzarella.

- **600g (1¼lb) mixed heirloom tomatoes, sliced**
- **2 large avocados (640g), sliced**
- **6 large fresh figs (480g), halved**
- **1 cup fresh basil leaves**
- **2 tablespoons caramelised balsamic vinegar**
- **2 tablespoons extra virgin olive oil**

RAW MOZZARELLA

- **¾ cup (115g) raw cashews**
- **½ cup (125ml) soy milk**
- **¼ cup (55g) coconut oil (see tips)**
- **¼ cup (60ml) lemon juice**
- **2 teaspoons nutritional yeast flakes**
- **2 teaspoons tahini**
- **2 teaspoons onion powder**
- **1 teaspoon garlic powder**
- **1 teaspoon sea salt flakes**
- **1 tablespoon psyllium husk powder**
- **½ cup (125ml) water**

1 Make raw mozzarella.

2 Slice half the mozzarella (reserve remaining for another use, see vegan hacks). Arrange mozzarella, tomatoes, avocado, figs and basil on a platter; season. Drizzle with vinegar and oil to serve.

raw mozzarella Oil a deep 1¾-cup bowl. Blend cashews, soy milk, coconut oil, lemon juice, nutritional yeast, tahini, onion powder, garlic powder and salt in a high-powered blender until smooth and creamy. Whisk psyllium and the water in a small bowl; stand for 5 minutes until thick and gel-like. Add psyllium mixture to cashew mixture; blend until smooth. Scrape mixture into oiled bowl, press down to remove any air bubbles. Cover with plastic wrap; refrigerate overnight or until firm.

tips Choose a coconut oil that has a mild coconut taste. The raw mozzarella will make 440g (14oz), drizzle any leftovers with olive oil and store it in an airtight container in the fridge for up to 1 week.

vegan hacks The mozzarella can also be melted and grilled so try it in toasted sandwiches or on pizza. Nutritional yeast flakes are available from health food stores; psyllium husk powder is available from health food stores and some major supermarkets. Yeast flakes will add a moreish savoury flavour to the mozzarella, while the psyllium powder will help bind. Remaining psyllium powder can be sprinkled into smoothies and on muesli. Leftover yeast flakes can be used as seasoning on almost anything.

Sweet dips & fruity dippers

PEANUT CARAMEL

PREP TIME 10 MINUTES (+ STANDING) **MAKES** 1¾ CUPS

Pit 1 cup fresh dates. Place in a small bowl with enough cold water to cover. Stand for 30 minutes; drain. Blend drained dates with ½ cup smooth peanut butter, ¼ cup coconut cream, ¼ cup melted coconut oil, 1 tablespoon pure maple syrup and ¼ teaspoon salt. Serve with pancakes or fresh fruit. Keep refrigerated in an airtight container for up to 2 weeks.

VANILLA FLUFF

PREP TIME 10 MINUTES (+ STANDING) **MAKES** 1½ CUPS

Place 1 cup raw cashews in a medium bowl with enough cold water to cover. Stand, covered for 4 hours or overnight. Drain cashews, rinse under cold water; drain well. Blend cashews with ¾ cup coconut cream, ¼ cup pure maple syrup, ¼ cup melted coconut oil and 2 teaspoons vanilla bean paste until as smooth as possible. Serve vanilla fluff as a dip with fresh fruit or like a cream with desserts and cakes. (The texture of the fluff improves after overnight refrigeration.) Keep refrigerated in an airtight container for up to 1 week.

Serve the dips with a selection of fruits for coating, spooning onto or scooping up with.

NOUGAT WHIP

PREP TIME 10 MINUTES (+ STANDING) **MAKES** 2 CUPS

Place 1¼ cups raw cashews in a medium bowl with enough cold water to cover. Stand, covered, for 4 hours. Drain cashews, rinse under cold water; drain well. Blend drained cashews with ½ cup coconut cream, ¼ cup pure maple syrup and ¼ cup almond butter until as smooth as possible. Add ¼ cup melted coconut oil and ½ teaspoons vanilla extract. Blend until as smooth as possible. Serve nougat whip with figs, cherries and other seasonal fruit, or use like a cream with desserts and cakes. (The texture of the whip improves after overnight refrigeration.) Keep refrigerated in an airtight container for up to 1 week.

MMM... CHOCOLATE

PREP TIME 10 MINUTES (+ STANDING) **MAKES** 1¼ CUPS

Bring a medium saucepan one-third filled with water to the boil. Remove from heat. Place a medium heatproof bowl over the pan. Add ¼ cup coconut oil and ¼ cup (50g) chopped cacao butter; whisk until combined and smooth. Whisk in ¼ cup pure maple syrup, then ⅔ cup sifted cacao powder. Serve sauce with strawberries for dipping or poured over vegan ice-cream. Keep refrigerated in an airtight container for up to 1 week. Mixture will firm on refrigeration; stir over a bowl of hot water to loosen, or microwave for a few seconds.

PREP TIME 45 MINUTES (+ FREEZING) **MAKES** 12

BLUEBERRY COCONUT BARS

Store these treats in an airtight container in the freezer for up to 1 month. Thaw before eating.

- **2½ cups (200g) desiccated coconut**
- **80g (2½oz) coconut butter, melted**
- **2 tablespoons coconut oil, melted**
- **¼ cup (18g) freeze-dried blueberry powder**
- **⅓ cup (80ml) coconut cream**
- **2 tablespoons pure maple syrup**
- **1 tablespoon desiccated coconut, extra**
- **½ teaspoon freeze-dried blueberry powder, extra**
- **fresh blueberries and dried rose petals, to decorate (optional)**

CHOCOLATE COATING

- **120g (4oz) cacao butter, chopped finely**
- **½ cup (115g) coconut oil**
- **¼ cup (60ml) pure maple syrup**
- **½ teaspoon vanilla extract**
- **1 cup (100g) cacao powder**

1 Grease a 12cm x 25cm (4¾in x 10in) top-measurement and 15cm x 27cm (6in x 10¾in) base-measurement loaf pan; line with plastic wrap, allowing excess to overhang sides.

2 Place desiccated coconut into a medium bowl. Rub in melted coconut butter and coconut oil, using fingertips, until mixture resembles breadcrumbs. Mix in blueberry powder, then coconut cream and maple syrup. Evenly press mixture into lined pan; freeze for 30 minutes or until firm.

3 Remove mixture from pan; trim edges and cut crossways into 12 bars. (If you like, round the corners of each bar using your hand and or a palette knife.) Place bars on a baking-paper-lined tray; freeze while making the chocolate coating.

4 Make chocolate coating.

5 Working with one at a time, dip bars in chocolate holding bars underneath with two forks. Gently shake off excess chocolate and return to tray. Freeze for 10 minutes until set.

6 Trim off any excess chocolate; double dip bars with any leftover chocolate. Return to freezer to set for 10 minutes and trim again.

7 Combine extra desiccated coconut and blueberry powder in a small bowl and sprinkle over bars in a line. Decorate with fresh blueberries and dried rose petals.

chocolate coating Place cacao butter, coconut oil, maple syrup and vanilla in a medium heatproof bowl over a smaller heatproof bowl of boiling water, whisk until combined. Whisk in cacao powder until combined and smooth.

tips If chocolate coating thickens, place bowl over hot water until melted. Bars will keep, stored in an airtight container in the freezer for up to 1 month. Remove from freezer 45 minutes before eating. These bars are best served at room temperature, so they can soften.

PREP TIME 1 HOUR 10 MINUTES (+ STANDING & REFRIGERATION) **SERVES** 16

STRAWBERRIES & CREAM UN-CHEESECAKE

You will need to start this recipe at least 1 day ahead to soak the cashews and to set the cake.

- **2½ cups (375g) raw cashews**
- **1 cup (140g) raw macadamias**
- **¾ cup (60g) desiccated coconut**
- **½ cup (60g) almond meal**
- **6 fresh dates (120g), pitted**
- **¼ teaspoon vanilla bean paste**
- **¾ cup (150g) coconut oil, melted**
- **400g (12½oz) small strawberries**
- **1 cup (240g) coconut yoghurt**
- **½ cup (125ml) light agave syrup**
- **1 tablespoon finely grated lemon rind**
- **⅓ cup (80ml) lemon juice**
- **½ teaspoon vanilla bean paste, extra**
- **80g (1½oz) cacao butter, melted**
- **halved extra strawberries, coconut flakes and edible flowers, to serve (optional)**

1 Place cashews in a medium bowl with enough cold water to cover. Stand, covered, for 4 hours. Drain, rinse under cold water; drain well.

2 Grease a 23cm (9in) round springform cake pan. Line base and side of pan with baking paper, extending the paper 5cm (2in) above edge of pan.

3 Process macadamias, desiccated coconut, almond meal, dates and vanilla paste until mixture resembles coarse crumbs. Add 1 tablespoon of the coconut oil; process until combined and mixture starts to stick together. Press mixture over base of pan, then using the back of a spoon, press down firmly and level.

4 Hull then thinly slice strawberries lengthways. Strawberries shouldn't be more than 3.5cm (1½in) tall, or the tips won't be covered by filling; trim strawberries if needed. Place tallest strawberry slices around side of cake pan, sticking them to the baking paper; reserve remaining slices. Refrigerate pan until required.

5 Blend drained cashews with coconut yoghurt, syrup, rind, juice and extra vanilla paste until as smooth as possible. Add cacao butter and remaining coconut oil; blend until as smooth as possible. Pour two-thirds of the mixture over the base; smooth the surface. Refrigerate while preparing strawberry layer.

6 Blend reserved strawberry slices until as smooth as possible; stir into the remaining cashew mixture. Gently spoon strawberry mixture over cream layer; do not pour or layers will combine. Refrigerate overnight or until set.

7 Remove cake from pan and place on a plate to serve. Top with halved extra strawberries, coconut flakes and edible flowers.

tips If you have one, use a high-powered blender in steps 5 and 6 to achieve a really smooth results. The cake will keep in an airtight container in the fridge for up to 4 days.

PREP TIME 30 MINUTES **SERVES** 4

CAULIFLOWER COUSCOUS

Wringing the cauliflower gives it a real couscous fluffiness and amplifies the nutty flavour.

- **1 small cauliflower (1kg)**
- **1 teaspoon sea salt flakes**
- **1 cup firmly packed fresh mint leaves, chopped coarsely**
- **1 cup firmly packed fresh coriander (cilantro) leaves, chopped coarsely**
- **1 cup firmly packed fresh flat-leaf parsley, chopped coarsely**
- **300g (9½oz) fresh peas, shelled**
- **1½ cups (150g) mung bean sprouts**
- **½ cup (90g) pitted sicilian green olives, halved**
- **½ cup (70g) slivered pistachios**
50g (1½oz) preserved lemon, pulp discarded, rind sliced thinly
- **¼ cup (60ml) extra virgin olive oil**
- **2 tablespoons lemon juice**
- **¼ teaspoon freshly ground black pepper**
- **¼ teaspoon sea salt flakes, extra**
- **mint leaves extra and lemon wedges, to serve**

MINT YOGHURT SAUCE

- **½ cup (140g) coconut yoghurt**
- **2 tablespoons finely chopped fresh mint leaves**
- **¼ cup (60ml) fresh lemon juice**

1 Make mint yoghurt sauce.

2 Cut cauliflower into florets. Working in batches, process cauliflower and salt, until it resembles a couscous-like consistency. Transfer to a clean tea towel, doubled piece of muslin or a nut bag; squeeze all the liquid out of the cauliflower.

3 Transfer cauliflower couscous to a large bowl; fluff with a fork. Add herbs, peas, mung bean sprouts, olives, three-quarters of the pistachios and the preserved lemon rind; mix until well combined.

4 Whisk olive oil, lemon juice, pepper and extra salt in a small bowl until well combined. Drizzle over cauliflower couscous; stir to combine. Sprinkle with remaining pistachios. Serve topped with extra mint leaves, lemon wedges and yoghurt sauce.

mint yoghurt sauce Process coconut yoghurt, mint and lemon juice in a small food processor until smooth. (Alternatively, mix all ingredients together in a small bowl.) Season to taste. (Makes ½ cup)

tip Preserved lemons are a North African specialty; available from delicatessens and specialty food shops. Use the rind only. Remove and discard the fleshy pulp; rinse the rind well under cold water before using to remove excess saltiness.

food swaps Use the same amount of crunchy sprout combo instead of mung bean sprouts. Use whole or chopped pistachios or another nut for the slivered pistachios.

PREP TIME 20 MINUTES (+ STANDING) **SERVES** 2

ZUCCHINI ZOODLES WITH CASHEW PESTO

If you would like to make your own vegan parmesan to go with the zoodles, see page 17.

- **4 large zucchini (600g)**
- **125g (4oz) mixed heirloom cherry tomatoes, halved**
- **¼ cup fresh basil leaves**
- **1 tablespoon pine nuts**
- **2 tablespoons vegan parmesan (see page 17)**

CASHEW PESTO

- **⅔ cup (100g) raw cashews**
- **1 cup firmly packed fresh basil leaves**
- **¼ cup (40g) pine nuts**
- **2 tablespoons lemon juice**
- **¼ cup (60ml) extra virgin olive oil**
- **2 teaspoons nutritional yeast flakes**
- **1 clove garlic, crushed**

1 Make cashew pesto.

2 Using a spiraliser or julienne peeler (see tips), cut zucchini into zoodles; place in a large bowl.

3 Add pesto and cherry tomatoes to bowl; toss to combine. Serve topped with basil leaves, pine nuts and vegan parmesan. Serve immediately.

cashew pesto Place cashews in a small bowl with enough cold water to cover. Stand for 2 hours. Drain, rinse under cold water; drain well. Process drained cashews with basil, pine nuts, lemon juice, olive oil, nutritional yeast and garlic until smooth. Season to taste. (Makes 1 cup)

keep it Store leftover pesto in an airtight container in the fridge for 1 week. Spread leftover pesto on toast or seeded crackers for a delicious snack.

tips To make zoodles, there are a few methods you can use. A spiraliser is a hand cranked machine designed to cut vegetables into noodles or ribbons. A julienne peeler, this looks like a wide bladed vegetable peeler with a serrated rather than straight blade. Both items are available from kitchenware shops. Alternatively, you could peel the zucchini into long ribbons, stack on top of one another and cut into long thin strips.

CHEAP VEGAN

PREP + COOK TIME 25 MINUTES **SERVES** 4

BLACKENED STICKY HOT DOGS WITH RED SAUERKRAUT

Whole individual eggplant replace the hot dog sausages in this vegan reinvention.

- **2 tablespoons dijon mustard**
- **2 tablespoons pure maple syrup**
- **1 teaspoon cumin seeds, toasted, ground (see tip)**
- **1 teaspoon sea salt flakes**
- **4 medium lebanese eggplant (240g)**
- **4 vegan long crusty bread rolls (320)**
- **½ cup (130g) hummus**
- **130g (4oz) red cabbage sauerkraut**
- **small mint leaves and extra dijon mustard, to serve (optional)**

1 Preheat a chargrill plate (or barbecue) over high heat.

2 Combine mustard, maple syrup, cumin and salt in a small bowl.

3 Cut a deep, long slit along the top of each eggplant, cutting three-quarters of the way down but not all the way through. Brush all over eggplant including the cut surfaces lightly with mustard mixture.

4 Reduce grill plate heat to medium; place eggplants on grill plate, cover with a medium heatproof bowl or foil. Cook, turning occasionally, brushing with remaining mustard mixture at each turn for 15 minutes or until eggplants are soft in the centre.

5 Cut a slit along the top of each bread roll. Divide hummus among rolls, top with eggplant, sauerkraut, mint leaves and extra mustard.

tip Toasting and grinding whole spices amplifies and freshens the flavour. Place cumin seeds in a frying pan over low-medium heat; stir until fragrant and toasted. Grind using a mortar and pestle. Alternatively, you can use 1 teaspoon ground cumin.

PREP + COOK TIME 55 MINUTES SERVES 2

PINEAPPLE & BLACK RICE STIR-FRY

Black rice gets it colour from the antioxidant anthocyanin that assists with brain function.

- 1 cup (210g) black rice
- ¼ cup (60ml) vegetable oil
- 4 green onions (scallions), sliced thinly on the diagonal
- 2 cloves garlic, sliced
- 20g (¾oz) fresh ginger, peeled, cut into matchsticks
- 1 baby pak choy (60g), quartered
- 100g (3oz) sugar snap peas, trimmed, halved lengthways
- 1 medium capsicum (bell pepper) (200g), sliced thinly
- ½ small ripe pineapple (250g), sliced thinly
- 2 tablespoons tamari
- 2 tablespoons fresh lime juice

1 Place rice in a large saucepan with 2 litres (8 cups) water; bring to the boil. Cook, covered, for 35 minutes or until tender. Drain well.

2 Heat oil in a wok over high heat; stir-fry green onion, garlic and ginger for 2 minutes. Add pak choy, sugar snap peas, capsicum and pineapple; stir-fry for 3 minutes. Add cooked rice, tamari and lime juice; stir-fry for 1 minute. Divide between bowls.

food swaps Use snow peas or green beans instead of the sugar snap peas, depending on which is the more affordable at the time of shopping. If fresh pineapple is unavailable, you can use canned sliced pineapple in juice that's been drained well. Use brown rice or red rice, if preferred.

vegan hack You could add chopped firm tofu or tempeh when you stir-fry the green onion.

serving ideas Top the stir-fry with coriander (cilantro) leaves and serve with sriracha.

PREP + COOK TIME 30 MINUTES SERVES 4

COCONUT, TOMATO & LENTIL SOUP

Save even more time and money and make a double batch of this comforting soup to freeze.

- **1 tablespoon coconut oil**
- **1 small onion (80g), sliced thinly**
- **2 teaspoons yellow mustard seeds**
- **2 teaspoons curry powder**
- **2 tablespoons tomato paste**
- **1 cup (150g) red lentils**
- **1 litre (4 cups) vegetable stock**
- **½ cup (125ml) coconut milk, plus extra to drizzle**
- **2 medium tomatoes (300g)**
- **fresh coriander (cilantro) leaves and lemon wedges, to serve**

1 Heat coconut oil in a medium saucepan over medium-high heat; cook onion, stirring, for 3 minutes or until soft. Add mustard seeds; stir for 4 minutes or until they start to pop. Add curry powder; cook, stirring, for 1 minute. Add tomato paste; cook, stirring, for a further 30 seconds.

2 Add lentils, vegetable stock and coconut milk; bring to the boil. Reduce heat to low; simmer, covered, for 10 minutes, stirring occasionally or until lentils are tender. Coarsely chop 1 fresh tomato; stir into soup until just heated through. Season to taste.

3 Ladle soup into bowls; drizzle with a little extra coconut milk, then top with remaining coarsely chopped fresh tomato and the coriander leaves. Serve with lemon wedges.

vegan hacks Turn this soup into a curry, by reducing the quantity of stock by 1 cup. You could also serve the soup topped with coarsely chopped smoked almonds or crushed pappadums.

keep it Soup can be frozen at the end of step 2. Freeze in airtight containers for up to 1 month.

PREP + COOK TIME 20 MINUTES SERVES 2

SOBA NOODLE BOWLS WITH CHILLI GARLIC SAUCE

Green beans, frozen peas and sugar snap peas can all be used in place of the edamame if you like.

- 3 green onions (scallions)
- ½ teaspoon dried chilli flakes
- 2 small cloves garlic, crushed
- 2 tablespoons tamari
- 2 tablespoons chinese black vinegar
- 2 tablespoons sesame oil
- 1 bunch choy sum (500g), trimmed, halved
- 180g (5½oz) dried green tea soba noodles
- 250g (8oz) frozen edamame (soybeans), thawed, shelled
- toasted sesame seeds, to serve (optional)

1 Cut 1 green onion into 6cm (2½in) lengths, then into long strips; place in a bowl of iced water to curl. Thinly slice remaining green onions.

2 Combine chilli flakes, garlic, tamari, vinegar, 1 tablespoon sesame oil and the sliced green onion in a small bowl.

3 Bring a saucepan of salted water to the boil over high heat. Cook choy sum for 1 minute or until tender and crisp. Remove with tongs; place on a plate and drizzle with remaining 1 tablespoon sesame oil.

4 Return the saucepan of water to the boil. Add noodles; cook for 3 minutes. Add edamame to noodles; cook for a further 1 minute or until noodles are tender and edamame heated through. Drain; return noodles and edamame to the pan. Add chilli garlic sauce; toss gently to combine.

5 Divide noodles and choy sum between bowls; top with green onion curls and sesame seeds.

vegan hacks If you can find shelled edamame you will need 120g (4oz).

PREP + COOK TIME 40 MINUTES SERVES 4

AFRICAN PEANUT STEW

Silver beet is a vegetable that provides great value and volume especially in the cooler months.

- 300g (9½oz) baby (chat) potatoes
- 1 bunch silver beet (swiss chard) (750g)
- 2 tablespoons extra virgin olive oil
- 1 tablespoon grated fresh ginger
- 1 clove garlic, crushed
- 1 medium onion (150g), peeled, cut into wedges
- 1 large orange sweet potato (500g), cut into 5cm (2in) cubes
- 1 teaspoon ground cumin
- 1 teaspoon dried chilli flakes
- 2 tablespoons tomato paste
- 1 cup (28g) natural crunchy peanut butter
- 2 cups (500ml) vegetable stock
- 2 tablespoons fresh lime juice
- ½ cup fresh coriander (cilantro)
- ½ cup (70g) roasted unsalted peanuts

1 Place baby potatoes in a medium saucepan with enough water to cover. Bring to the boil over high heat; boil for 6 minutes or until par-cooked. Drain. Meanwhile, separate silver beet stems from stalks and thinly slice. Tear leaves into pieces.

2 Heat 1 tablespoon of the oil in a large saucepan over medium-high heat; cook ginger, garlic and onion for 2 minutes. Add sweet potato; cook, stirring, for 5 minutes or until lightly golden. Add cumin, chilli flakes and tomato paste; cook for 1 minute.

3 Add peanut butter, stock and 1¼ cups (310ml) water; stir until peanut butter is combined. Add par-cooked potatoes and silver beet stems; bring to the boil. Reduce heat; simmer, covered, for 12 minutes, stirring occasionally to prevent sticking, or until potatoes are tender. Remove from heat; stir in lime juice.

4 Just before serving, heat remaining oil in a large frying pan. Cook silver beet leaves for 3 minutes or until wilted. Season to taste.

5 Serve curry immediately, topped with wilted silver beet leaves, coriander and peanuts.

serving ideas Top the stew with fresh red chilli for extra kick; serve with brown rice and lime wedges

PREP + COOK TIME 15 MINUTES **MAKES** 4

MUSHROOM & SPINACH GOZLEME

If you have one, you can cook these super-easy mountain bread gozleme in a sandwich press.

- **⅓ cup (80ml) extra virgin olive oil**
- **1 small onion (80g), chopped finely**
- **2 cloves garlic, crushed**
- **2 teaspoons ground cumin**
- **2 teaspoons ground sumac**
- **½ teaspoon chilli flakes**
- **350g (11oz) flat mushrooms, sliced thickly**
- **100g (3oz) vegan cheddar, grated**
- **60g (2oz) spinach leaves**
- **2 tablespoons pine nuts, toasted**
- **4 mountain bread wraps (100g)**
- **olive oil cooking spray**
- **mint leaves and lemon wedges, to serve**

1 Heat 1 tablespoon of the oil in a large frying pan over high; cook onion and garlic, stirring, for 5 minutes or until softened. Stir in cumin, sumac and chilli flakes; cook for 1 minute. Transfer mixture to a bowl.

2 Heat 1½ tablespoons of the oil in same frying pan. Add half the mushrooms; cook, turning occasionally, for 5 minutes or until golden. Add cooked mushrooms to onion mixture. Repeat with remaining oil and mushrooms. Cool combined mixture for 10 minutes. Stir in vegan cheddar, spinach and pine nuts; season to taste.

3 Heat a large frying pan over high heat. Place two mountain bread wraps on a work bench. Spread a quarter of the filling mixture down the centre third of each wrap. Fold both sides over to enclose. Spray with olive oil cooking spray. Cook in the pan for 2 minutes each side or until cheddar melts and bread is crisp. Remove from pan, using a large spatula. Cover to keep warm. Repeat with remaining mountain bread wraps and filling, spraying with olive oil.

4 Cut each gozleme diagonally and serve with mint and lemon wedges.

PREP + COOK TIME 45 MINUTES **SERVES** 4

EGGPLANT & CHICKPEA YELLOW CURRY

Roasting the eggplant first gives this curry a wonderful depth of flavour from few ingredients.

- **2½ tablespoons yellow curry powder**
- **¼ cup (60ml) vegetable oil**
- **6 japanese eggplants (500g), cut into 2cm (¾in) wedges**
- **6 apple eggplants (300g), halved**
- **1 cup (200g) brown rice**
- **3 shallots, sliced**
- **400g (12½oz) can chickpeas (garbanzo beans), drained, rinsed**
- **400ml can coconut milk**
- **1 cup (250ml) vegetable stock**
- **½ cup fresh thai basil leaves**
- **1 tablespoon lemon juice**
- **toasted coconut flakes and sliced red chiili, to serve**

1 Preheat oven to 200°C/400°F. Line a medium roasting pan with baking paper.

2 Combine 2 teaspoon of the curry powder and 2 tablespoons of the oil in roasting pan, add eggplants; toss to coat. Season. Roast for 30 minutes or until eggplants are tender.

3 Meanwhile, place brown rice and 2 cups (500ml) water in a saucepan over medium heat; bring to a simmer. Reduce heat to low; cook, covered, for 25 minutes or until rice is tender and water is absorbed.

4 Heat remaining oil in a large, deep frying pan over medium heat; cook shallots for 3 minutes or until soft. Add remaining 2 tablespoons curry powder; cook, stirring, for 2 minutes. Add chickpeas, coconut milk, stock and three-quarters of the thai basil. Bring to a simmer; cook for a further 5 minutes or until slightly reduced.

5 Add roasted eggplant to curry with lemon juice; stir until warmed through. Serve with brown rice and top with remaining thai basil leaves, coconut flakes and chilli.

tip We used a mild yellow curry powder containing coriander seeds, paprika, turmeric, cumin, fennel, ginger, cassia, chilli and cardamom.

food swap If you can't find japanese and apple eggplants, use 800g (1½lb) regular eggplant cut into 4cm (1½in) pieces instead.

Fried rice

EXTRA VEG FRIED RICE

PREP + COOK TIME 20 MINUTES **SERVES** 2

From 1 bunch gai lan, coarsely chop leaves and stems, keeping each part separate. Drain and pat dry 200g (6½oz) silken tofu, then slice. Heat 2 teaspoons each vegetable and sesame oil in a wok; stir-fry tofu for 3 minutes or until crisp and broken up. Remove from wok. Stir-fry 1 finely chopped onion, carrot, capsicum (bell pepper) and 10 snow peas for 2 minutes or until softened. Add gai lan stalks; stir-fry for 2 minutes. Remove from wok. Heat 1 tablespoon vegetable oil and 2 teaspoons sesame oil in wok. Add 250g (4oz) packet microwave brown rice and 1 teaspoon chinese five spice powder; stir-fry for 3 minutes or until heated through. Stir in vegetables, gai lan leaves, tofu and 2 tablespoons tamari. Serve with sriracha.

KIMCHI FRIED RICE

PREP + COOK TIME 15 MINUTES **SERVES** 2

Thinly slice 6 green onions, keeping white part and green part separate. Reserve a small handful of green onion to serve. Heat 2 tablespoons vegetable oil and 3 teaspoons sesame oil in a wok over medium-high heat. Stir-fry white part of onion and 2 teaspoons korean red pepper paste (gochungung) for 1 minute. Add 2 x 250g (4oz) packets microwave short-grain rice; stir-fry for 5 minutes or until heated through. Add 1 cup chopped kimchi, ½ cup shelled thawed edamame (soybeans) and green part of onions; stir-fry until heated through. Serve topped with reserved green onion, a handful of bean sprouts and purchased toasted sesame nori crisps.

CHICKEN-LIKE FRIED RICE

PREP + COOK TIME 20 MINUTES **SERVES** 2

Split 1 bunch broccolini in half lenthways. Cut a 200g (6½oz) block tempeh into small cubes. Combine 2 tablespoons each tamari, rice wine vinegar and sriracha in a bowl. Heat 1 tablespoon vegetable oil in a wok over medium heat; stir-fry tempeh for 5 minutes or until golden on all sides. Remove from wok; keep warm. Add 250g (4oz) microwave long-grain white rice; stir-fry until heated through. Remove from wok; keep warm. Add broccolini and ½ cup frozen peas to wok; stir-fry until bright green. Return rice to wok with tamari mixture; toss to combine. Serve topped with tempeh, sliced long red chilli and lime wedges.

TOM YUM FRIED RICE

PREP + COOK TIME 20 MINUTES **SERVES** 2

Trim 400g (12½oz) green beans; halve lengthways. Wash 1 bunch fresh coriander (cilantro), paying attention to roots. Pick leaves from coriander; you need 1 cup. Coarsely chop coriander stems and roots; you need ½ cup. Heat 2 tablespoons vegetable oil in a wok over high heat; fry 200g (6½oz) sliced firm tofu for 2 minutes on each side or until golden. Remove from wok; keep warm. Stir-fry ¼ cup vegan tom yum paste and coriander stem and root mix for 3 minutes or until fragrant. Add beans, 125g (4oz) cherry tomatoes and 2 x 250g (4oz) packets microwave jasmine rice; stir-fry for 3 minutes or until rice is heated through and beans are tender. Serve topped with tofu, reserved coriander leaves and lime cheeks.

PREP + COOK TIME 1 HOUR (+ REFRIGERATION) **SERVES** 4

SPAGHETTI WITH 'MEATBALLS'

These meatballs are powered by the incredibly satisfying and hearty taste of mushrooms.

- ¼ cup (60ml) olive oil
- 1 large onion (200g), chopped finely
- 600g (1¼lb) swiss brown mushrooms, chopped finely
- ⅓ cup (80ml) olive oil, extra
- 4 cloves garlic, crushed
- 2 teaspoons dried oregano
- 1 cup (100g) fresh breadcrumbs
- ⅔ cup (60g) rolled oats
- 400g (12½oz) can chickpeas (garbanzo beans), drained, rinsed
- 25g (¾oz) dried shiitake mushrooms, grated (see tip)
- ⅓ cup finely chopped fresh flat-leaf parsley
- ¼ cup (40g) plain (all-purpose) flour
- 400g (12½oz) spaghetti

MARINARA SAUCE

- 2 tablespoons olive oil
- 1 large onion (200g), chopped finely
- 4 cloves garlic, crushed
- 1 fresh long red chilli, seeded, chopped finely
- 1 teaspoon dried oregano
- ½ cup (125ml) dry white wine
- 3 x 400g (12½oz) cans crushed tomatoes

1 Heat oil in a large frying pan over high heat; cook onion for 4 minutes or until golden. Add chopped mushrooms and 2 tablespoons of the extra oil; cook for 10 minutes or until all liquid has evaporated and mushrooms are golden.

2 Add garlic and oregano; cook for a further minute. Remove from heat; cool for 5 minutes. In a food processor, pulse mushroom mixture with breadcrumbs, oats, chickpeas, shiitakes and ¼ cup of the parsley until combined. Season to taste, then pulse until mixture is pasty.

3 Dust a large tray with half the flour. Using lightly damp hands, roll heaped tablespoonfuls of mixture into 24 balls; place 'meatballs' on floured tray. Sift remaining flour over meatballs. Refrigerate, uncovered, for 2 hours or until firm.

4 Meanwhile, make marinara sauce.

5 Heat remaining 2 tablespoons of extra olive oil in a large, non-stick frying pan over medium heat. Cook meatballs, in batches, for 6 minutes, gently shaking pan occasionally, until evenly browned. Add marinara to pan; toss very gently to combine and warm through, taking care not to break up meatballs.

6 Meanwhile, cook spaghetti in a large saucepan of boiling water for 12 minutes or until almost tender; drain.

7 Serve spaghetti topped with meatball mixture and sprinkled with remaining parsley.

marinara sauce Heat olive oil in a medium saucepan over medium heat; cook onion for 4 minutes or until softened. Add garlic, chilli and oregano; cook for a further minute or until fragrant. Increase heat to high. Add wine; cook for a minute or until evaporated. Add tomatoes; bring to the boil. Reduce heat to medium; simmer for 15 minutes or until thickened slightly. Season to taste.

tip Use a microplane grater to finely grate the dried shiitake mushrooms; alternatively, you can ground them to a fine powder using a high-powered spice grinder or blender.

serving idea Serve sprinkled with vegan parmesan (to make your own, see page 17).

BOLLYWOOD TOFU KEBABS WITH MINT YOGHURT SAUCE

Check the back label of the coconut yoghurt as sugar is not always declared on the front label.

- 500g (1lb) firm tofu
- 1 medium red capsicum (bell pepper) (200g)
- 1 medium red onion (170g)
- 2 medium tomatoes (300g)
- 2 tablespoons tandoori paste
- ⅓ cup (95g) coconut yoghurt
- 1 tablespoon small fresh mint leaves
- lime wedges, to serve

MINT YOGHURT SAUCE

- ½ cup (140g) coconut yoghurt
- 2 tablespoons finely chopped fresh mint leaves
- ¼ cup (60ml) fresh lime juice

1 Preheat an oiled barbecue flat plate. Soak four bamboo skewers in cold water to prevent them scorching.

2 Pat tofu dry well with paper towel, then cut into 2cm x 4cm (¾in x 1½in) pieces. Remove seeds from capsicum. Cut capsicum and red onion into eight 4cm (1½in) pieces. Cut tomatoes into quarters.

3 Combine paste and coconut yoghurt in a medium bowl. Add tofu; stir gently until evenly coated.

4 Thread vegetables and tofu, alternating, onto skewers. Cook, kebabs, for 5 minutes each side or until vegetables are tender and tofu is golden.

5 Make mint yoghurt sauce.

6 Serve kebabs with sauce, mint leaves and lime wedges.

mint yoghurt sauce Process coconut yoghurt, mint and lime juice in a small food processor until smooth. (Alternatively, mix ingredients together in a small bowl.) (Makes ½ cup)

tips These kebabs are a little on the spicy side, you may want to adjust the quantity of tandoori paste if you prefer less spicy tastes. You can also cook the kebabs in 220°C/425°F oven for 30 minutes, turning over halfway through the cooking time, or until browned.

PREP + COOK TIME 50 MINUTES **MAKES** 8

SWEET POTATO & PEA SAMOSAS

You can also make the samosas with regular potatoes or use a mix of both potato types.

- **500g (1lb) orange sweet potatoes, peeled, cut into 1cm (½in) cubes**
- **2 tablespoons coconut oil, melted**
- **½ medium onion (75g), chopped finely**
- **2 teaspoons grated fresh ginger**
- **2 teaspoons curry powder**
- **1 cup (120g) frozen peas**
- **⅓ cup (50g) sunflower seeds**
- **12 sheets fillo pastry (180g)**
- **½ teaspoon cumin seeds**
- **½ teaspoon salt flakes**

MINT APPLE RAITA

- **½ cup fresh mint leaves**
- **¼ teaspoon sea salt flakes**
- **1 cup (280g) coconut yoghurt**
- **1 small green apple (130g), cut into julienne**

1 Preheat oven to 200°C/400°F. Line an oven tray with baking paper.

2 Place sweet potato in a medium saucepan with enough water to cover; bring to boil over high heat. Boil for 5 minutes or until tender. Drain well.

3 Heat half the coconut oil in a frying pan over medium heat; cook, onion, ginger and curry powder, stirring, for 3 minutes or until fragrant and softened. Add sweet potato and peas; cook, stirring, for 1 minute or until the liquid evaporates. Stir in sunflower seeds; season to taste. Cool.

4 Brush 1 sheet of fillo with a little of the remaining coconut oil, fold in half lengthways, then brush with a little more coconut oil. Place ⅓ cup sweet potato mixture at the bottom of one narrow edge of folded pastry sheet. Fold one corner of pastry diagonally over filling for form a triangle. Continue folding to the end of the pastry sheet, retaining the triangular shape. Place on tray; brush with a little more coconut oil. Repeat with remaining fillo, coconut oil and filling mixture to make a total of 8 samosas. Sprinkle with cumin seeds and salt.

5 Bake samosas for 15 minutes or until golden and crisp.

6 Make mint apple raita.

7 Serve samosas warm with raita.

mint apple raita Using a mortar and pestle, pound mint leaves and salt to a smooth paste. Stir through coconut yoghurt and apple. Thin if necessary with a little water if yoghurt is thick. Season with pepper.

tips Use olive oil if you prefer instead of coconut oil. You can also cook the samosas in a flat sandwich press, for 2 minutes or until crisp and lightly golden.

serving idea Serve samosas with lemon wedges.

CHILL
OUT

PREP + COOK TIME 1 HOUR **SERVES** 4

LOADED ROOT VEGETABLE FRIES WITH BEER & MUSTARD SAUCE

The secret to irresistible crisp fries is to ensure that they are spread in a single layer on oven trays.

- **500g (1lb) sebago potatoes**
- **300g (9½oz) purple sweet potatoes**
- **300g (9½oz) orange sweet potatoes**
- **300g (9½oz) parsnips**
- **½ cup (125ml) vegetable oil**
- **2 tablespoons sea salt flakes**
- **1 bunch fresh chives, chopped finely**

BEER & MUSTARD SAUCE

- **25g (¾oz) vegan butter-style spread**
- **2 tablespoons plain (all-purpose) flour**
- **1 cup (250ml) pale ale**
- **½ cup (125ml) almond milk**
- **1 tablespoon wholegrain mustard**
- **¼ teaspoon cayenne pepper**
- **1 teaspoon vegan worcestershire sauce (see vegan hack)**
- **1⅓ cup (160g) vegan cheddar**
- **½ cup (50g) vegan mozzarella**

1 Preheat oven 220°C/425°F. Line three large oven trays with baking paper.

2 Scrub all potatoes and the parsnips. Cut unpeeled potatoes into 5mm (¼in) wide shoestring chips and parsnips into 1cm (¾in) wide wedges. Place potatoes and parsnips in a clean tea towel; gently squeeze to remove excess moisture.

3 Divide vegetables, oil and salt among oven trays; toss to coat. Spread out evenly in a single layer. Roast, turning halfway, for 35 minutes or until fries are golden and crisp.

4 Meanwhile, make beer and mustard sauce.

5 Serve fries with sauce, sprinkled with chives.

beer & mustard sauce Melt spread in a medium saucepan over medium heat. Add flour; stir for 1 minute to a smooth paste. Gradually stir in combined beer, almond milk and mustard; cook, stirring, for 5 minutes or until mixture boils and thickens. Add cayenne, worcestershire sauce and vegan cheeses; stir mixture until cheeses melt.

tip The sauce will thicken on standing; keep warm until required. Stir in a little extra almond milk if you need to thin it down a little.

vegan hack Vegan worcestershire sauce is available from some major supermarkets and online; check the brand label carefully to ensure it does not contain anchovies. If unavailable, use tamari instead.

PREP + COOK TIME 10 MINUTES (+ FREEZING & REFRIGERATION) **SERVES** 2

BIRTHDAY CAKE MYLKSHAKE

You will need to freeze the bananas and refrigerate the coconut cream a day ahead.

- **2 large bananas (460g), chopped**
- **270ml can coconut cream, unopened (see tip)**
- **1 cup (250ml) unsweetened vanilla almond milk**
- **2 tablespoons cashew butter**
- **2 tablespoons vegan vanilla protein powder (see vegan hacks)**
- **2 tablespoons pure maple syrup**
- **2 teaspoons vanilla extract**
- **½ teaspoon natural pink food colouring (optional)**
- **1½ tablespoons vegan rainbow sprinkles and jimmies (see vegan hacks)**

1 Freeze bananas in an airtight container overnight. Refrigerate unopened can of coconut cream overnight.

2 Open the can of coconut cream; scrape the thick cream from the top of the can into a small bowl. Pour the remaining coconut cream into a high-powered blender. Add frozen banana, almond milk, cashew butter, protein powder, maple syrup, 1 teaspoon vanilla and the colouring; blend until smooth. Stir through 1 tablespoon sprinkles. Pour into two tall glasses.

3 Add remaining vanilla to thick coconut cream in bowl; whisk with an electric mixer until thick and fluffy. Spoon into a piping bag fitted with a fluted nozzle, pipe onto mylkshakes. Decorate with remaining sprinkles.

tip You will need a brand of pure coconut cream without stabilisers to make it homogenised, otherwise the coconut cream will not have two distinct layers; a thick top layer and a thin cream underneath.

vegan hacks There are many forms of protein powder, vegans need to look for those made from pea protein. Check the ingredients listed on the rainbow sprinkles as some contain gelatine derived from animal sources.

PREP + COOK TIME 35 MINUTES (+ STANDING) **SERVES** 8 (MAKES 32 BITES)

WARM PRETZEL BITES WITH MAPLE MUSTARD DIP

Bites can be made up to 8 hours ahead; reheat in the oven. The dip can be made the day before.

- **2 teaspoons coconut sugar**
- **1 teaspoon (4g) dried yeast**
- **1½ tablespoons coconut oil, melted**
- **¾ teaspoon sea salt flakes**
- **1¾ cups (265g) plain (all-purpose) flour**
- **2 tablespoons bicarbonate of soda (baking soda)**
- **3 teaspoons pink himalayan rock salt, crushed lightly**

MAPLE MUSTARD DIP

- **⅓ cup (100g) vegan mayonnaise (just like mayo, see page 17)**
- **1½ tablespoons dijon mustard**
- **1½ tablespoons pure maple syrup**
- **½ teaspoon Tabasco, plus extra to serve**

1 Combine coconut sugar, yeast and ¾ cup (180ml) warm water in a large bowl. Stand for 10 minutes or until mixture is foamy.

2 Preheat oven to 220°C/425°F. Line two large oven trays with baking paper.

3 Add coconut oil and salt flakes to yeast mixture. Add flour; mix to form a dough. Turn out onto a lightly floured surface; knead for 5 minutes or until smooth and elastic. Shape dough into a ball; place in an oiled bowl. Cover; stand in a warm place for 20 minutes or until risen slightly.

4 Divide dough into eight pieces. Roll each piece of dough out on a lightly floured suface. Roll each piece into a 15cm (6in) log; cut each log into four for a total of 32 bites.

5 Bring 1.25 litres (5 cups) water to the boil in a medium saucepan. Remove from heat, stir in bicarbonate of soda. Dip pretzel bites, in batches, in the bicarbonate of soda water for 30 seconds. Remove with a slotted spoon; place on lined trays. While pretzels are still wet, sprinkle with rock salt.

6 Bake pretzel bites for 12 minutes or until golden brown.

7 Make maple mustard dip.

8 Serve warm pretzel bites with dip.

maple mustard dip Whisk ingredients in a small bowl until combined. Serve with a drop of extra Tabasco on top, if you like.

food swap Sprinkle the bites with sea salt flakes instead of himalayan rock salt.

PREP + COOK TIME 30 MINUTES (+ FREEZING) MAKES 8

COCONUT CHOC TOPS

You will need to make the coconut 'nice cream' a day ahead, before filling and dipping the tops.

- **800ml canned coconut milk**
- **½ cup (85g) unrefined sugar (see tips)**
- **½ teaspoon sea salt flakes**
- **2 teaspoons vanilla bean paste**
- **8 ice-cream cone cups (30g)**
- **sprinkles, coconut flakes, freeze-dried raspberries and edible flowers, to decorate (optional)**

CHOCOLATE TOPPING

- **½ cup (65g) dutch-processed cocoa, sifted**
- **⅔ cup (150g) coconut oil, melted, cooled**
- **⅓ cup (80ml) pure maple syrup**

1 Blend coconut milk, sugar, salt and vanilla paste in a high-powered blender for 2 minutes or until sugar dissolves. (Alternatively whisk ingredients together in a medium bowl until sugar dissolves.) Transfer mixture to a large zip-top bag. Freeze overnight until firm.

2 Remove frozen coconut milk mixture from bag to the bowl of a food processor; pulse to break up ice crystals, until smooth. Transfer to an airtight container; freeze for 4 hours or overnight until firm.

3 When ready to serve, make chocolate topping.

4 Remove ice-cream from freezer; stand 5 minutes to soften slightly. Using an ice-cream scoop dipped in hot water, scoop balls of ice-cream into cone cups. Dip ice-cream into chocolate topping to coat. Stand in jars or glasses to keep upright (topping sets immediately); scatter with decorations if using. Store in the freezer until ready to serve.

chocolate topping Blend ingredients until mixture is as smooth as possible. Transfer to a small bowl or jug.

tips We used maple sugar, which is made from the sap of the maple tree and has a maple-like flavour. You can use brown sugar or coconut sugar instead. If you are decorating with sprinkles or any of the other suggested toppers, add them immediately after dipping the ice-creams in chocolate, before the topping sets too hard.

do-ahead Coconut choc tops can be assembled up to a day ahead; store in the freezer.

Popcorn flavours

CHEEZE SUPREME POPCORN

PREP + COOK TIME 10 MINUTES **SERVES** 4

Combine ¼ cup olive oil, 2 tablespoons nutritional yeast flakes, ½ teaspoon ground turmeric, 1 teaspoon onion powder and ½ teaspoon each smoked paprika and garlic powder in a large bowl. Heat 2 tablespoons olive oil in a large saucepan over medium heat. Add ½ cup popping corn, cover. Cook, shaking the pan occasionally, for 5 minutes or until the popping stops. Tip into the bowl; stir to coat.

VANILLA POPCORN WITH PEANUT BUTTER CARAMEL

PREP + COOK TIME 10 MINUTES **SERVES** 4

Combine ¼ cup each crunchy natural peanut butter and pure maple syrup in a small bowl. Heat 2 tablespoons olive oil in a large saucepan over medium heat. Add ½ cup popping corn and 1 teaspoon vanilla extract, cover. Cook, shaking the pan occasionally, for 5 minutes or until the popping stops. Tip into a bowl; add ½ cup roasted salted peanuts then drizzle with peanut butter caramel to coat.

MEXICAN CHURROS POPCORN

PREP + COOK TIME 10 MINUTES **SERVES** 4

Combine ¼ cup icing (confectioners') sugar, 2 tablespoons coconut sugar, 1 tablespoon ground cinnamon, ½ teaspoon ground allspice and ½ teaspoon sea salt flakes in a large bowl. Heat 2 tablespoons olive oil in a large saucepan over medium heat. Add ½ cup popping corn, cover. Cook, shaking the pan occasionally, for 5 minutes or until the popping stops. Tip into the bowl; stir to coat.

SALTED CHOCOLATE POPCORN

PREP + COOK TIME 15 MINUTES **SERVES** 4

Stir 1 tablespoon rosemary leaves, 1 teaspoon sea salt flakes, ¼ cup pepitas (pumpkin seed kernels) and ¼ cup vegan margarine in a small frying pan for 3 minutes or until margarine melts and seeds are lightly toasted. Cool. Pulse 100g (3oz) vegan dark chocolate in a food processor until finely chopped. Heat 2 tablespoons vegan margarine in a large saucepan over medium heat. Add ½ cup popping corn, cover. Cook, shaking the pan occasionally, for 5 minutes or until the popping stops. Add chopped chocolate and seed mixture to the pan; stir until chocolate melts and coats popcorn. Spread out onto a baking-paper-lined oven tray. Refrigerate for 5 minutes or until chocolate is set.

PREP + COOK TIME 15 MINUTES (+ FREEZING) **SERVES** 8

POPCORN ROCKY ROAD BARK

Coconut oil has a low melting point and the syrup keeps the bark soft so eat them while still frozen.

- **½ cup (100g) coconut oil**
- **½ cup (50g) cacao powder**
- **½ cup (120g) rice malt syrup**
- **1 tablespoon almond butter**
- **2 teaspoons vanilla extract**
- **1½ cups (25g) salted natural popcorn**
- **1 cup (50g) flaked coconut**
- **¾ cup (125g) dry-roasted almonds**
- **⅓ cup (45g) dried sweetened cranberries**

1 Line a 10cm x 20cm (4in x 8in) loaf pan with baking paper, extending the paper 2cm (¾in) above the edge.

2 Melt coconut oil in a medium saucepan over low heat. Remove from heat; whisk in cacao, rice malt syrup, almond butter and vanilla until cacao is dissolved and mixture is smooth.

3 Stir in three-quarters each of the popcorn, flaked coconut, almonds and cranberries. Spoon mixture into pan; spread evenly over base. Scatter with remaining popcorn, flaked coconut, almonds and cranberries; press lightly into cocoa mixture to secure.

4 Freeze bark for 15 minutes or until frozen solid.

5 Cut frozen bark into slices or chunks. Eat immediately frozen, or store in an airtight container in the freezer for up to 1 month.

food swaps You can use freeze-dried strawberries or raspberries instead of the cranberries.

PREP + COOK TIME 30 MINUTES **SERVES** 4

WASABI EDAMAME HUMMUS PLATTER

This is a brilliant way to whip up a sharing platter that looks impressive without too much effort.

- **1 cup (200g) frozen shelled edamame (soybeans)**
- **400g (12½oz) can chickpeas (garbanzo beans), drained, rinsed**
- **¼ cup (60ml) lime juice**
- **2 tablespoons tahini**
- **1½ teaspoons wasabi paste**
- **1 small clove garlic, crushed**
- **black sesame seeds, extra, to serve (optional)**

SESAME CRISPS

- **12 x 13cm (5¼in) frozen spring roll wrappers (see tips)**
- **cooking oil spray**
- **2 teaspoons black sesame seeds**
- **1 teaspoon sea salt flakes**

QUICK PICKLED VEG

- **¾ cup (180ml) rice wine vinegar**
- **½ cup (125ml) pure maple syrup**
- **¼ cup (60ml) soy sauce**
- **6 radishes (210g), quartered**
- **6 baby cucumbers (180g), quartered lengthways**

1 Make sesame crisps and quick pickled veg.

2 Place edamame in colander; place under running hot water until completely thawed. Drain well.

3 Reserve 1 tablespoon edamame for serving. Place remaining edamame in a food processor with chickpeas, lime juice, tahini, wasabi, garlic and ¼ cup (60ml) water; process until smooth. Season to taste.

4 Spoon dip into a serving bowl; top with reserved edamame, extra sesame seeds and drizzle with a little olive oil, if you like. Place dip on a platter with sesame crisps and pickled veg.

sesame crisps Preheat oven to 180°C /350°F. Line two oven trays with baking paper. Spray half the spring roll wrappers with oil, top with a second sheet; cut in half to make 12 rectangles. Place rectangles on lined trays; spray with oil, then sprinkle with sesame seeds and salt. Bake for 10 minutes or until golden. Cool. Break into shards for dipping.

quick pickled veg Stir vinegar, maple syrup and soy sauce in a small saucepan until almost simmering. Place radishes and cucumbers in a medium heatproof bowl; pour vinegar mixture over vegetables. Cover; refrigerate for 20 minutes.

tips You will find spring roll wrappers in the freezer section of the supermarket. Thaw before using. Quick pickled veg is best made on day of serving.

PREP + COOK TIME 50 MINUTES (+ REFRIGERATION) **SERVES** 4

FAUX GRAS WITH RED ONION JAM

Fortunately no animals were hurt in the making of this luscious mushroom pâté.

- 20g (¾oz) dried porcini mushrooms
- 1 cup (250ml) water
- ½ cup (125ml) brandy
- ¼ cup (60ml) olive oil
- 2 shallots, sliced thinly
- 200g (6½oz) fresh shiitake mushrooms, sliced thinly
- 200g (6oz) swiss brown mushrooms, sliced thinly
- 2 cloves garlic, crushed
- 2 tablespoons fresh thyme leaves, chopped finely
- ⅓ cup (80g) vegan cashew cheese
- chargrilled sourdough and extra thyme sprigs, to serve

RED ONION JAM

- 2 tablespoons olive oil
- 2 large red onions (600g), sliced thinly
- 1 tablespoon balsamic vinegar
- 1 tablespoon brown sugar

1 Bring porcini, the water and brandy to the boil in a small saucepan. Reduce heat to medium; simmer for 10 minutes or until mushrooms have softened. Strain mushrooms over a small heatproof bowl; reserve cooking liquid. Finely chop mushrooms.

2 Heat oil in a medium saucepan over medium heat; cook shallots for 5 minutes or until golden. Increase heat to high, add fresh mushrooms; cook for 6 minutes or until golden and dry. Stir in chopped porcini, garlic and thyme. Cook for 1 minute or until fragrant.

3 Add reserved cooking liquid; cook over high heat for 2 minutes or until all liquid has been absorbed.

4 Process mushroom mixture in a small food processor with cashew cheese until mixture forms an almost smooth paste with some texture. Season to taste. Transfer to a 3-cup (750ml) dish; refrigerate, covered for at least 30 minutes or until set.

5 Meanwhile, make red onion jam.

6 Serve faux gras on chargrilled sourdough with onion jam and extra thyme sprigs.

red onion jam Heat oil in a medium frying pan over high heat; cook onions for 2 minutes or until beginning to soften. Reduce heat to low; cook, stirring occasionally, for 20 minutes or until soft and golden. Increase heat to high, add vinegar and sugar; stir for 1 minute or until caramelised. Cool.

do-ahead Faux gras and onion jam can be made a day ahead; store, covered in the fridge. Bring to room temperature before serving.

Beauty masks

PREP TIME 15 MINUTES **MAKES** 2 MASKS

Place 2 teaspoons loose green tea in a mug, pour over ½ cup boiling water; steep for 10 minutes. Stir in 1 teaspoon lemon juice. Place ½ cup rice flour in a small food processor; strain green tea mixture over rice flour, blend to form a paste. Add ½ ripe avocado; blend until smooth. To use, spread half the mask on clean face and neck; leave on for 20 minutes. Rinse mask off with warm water then pat face dry. Place remaining mask in a small container or jar; cover the surface directly with plastic wrap and seal with a lid. Mask will keep in the fridge for up to 3 days.

PREP TIME 15 MINUTES **MAKES** 2 MASKS

Peel ¼ papaya (220g), remove and discard the seeds. Cut papaya into chunks; place in a food processor with 2 teaspoons white chia seeds and 1 tablespoon melted coconut oil. Blend until smooth; stand for 5 minutes or until mask has thickened. To use, spread half the mask on clean face and neck; leave for 20 minutes. Rinse mask off with warm water then pat face dry. Place remaining mask in a small container or jar; cover the surface directly with plastic wrap and seal with a lid. Mask will keep in the fridge for up to 3 days.

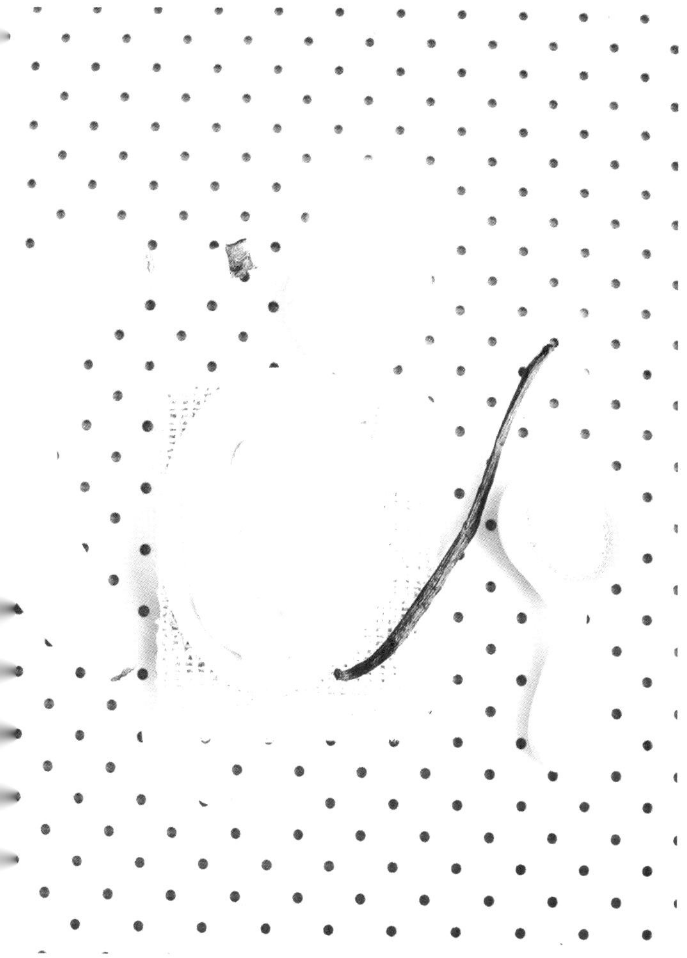

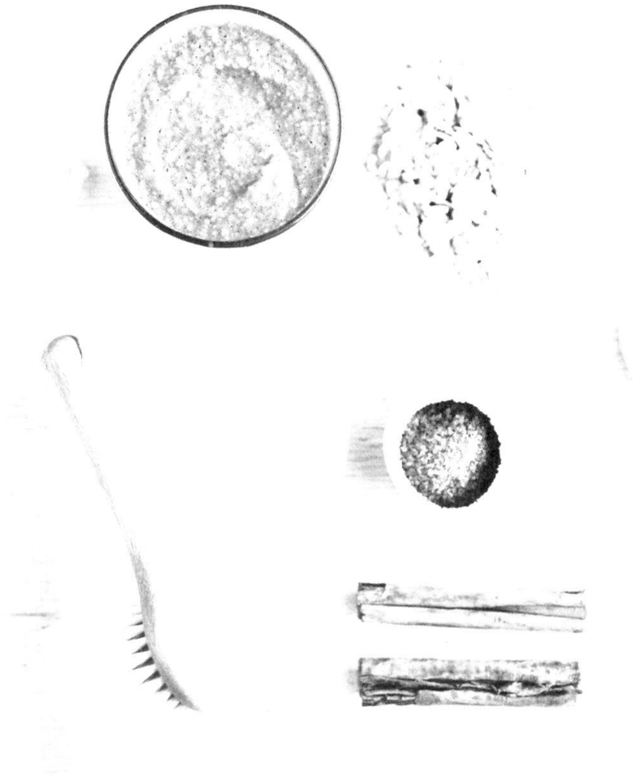

PREP TIME 5 MINUTES **MAKES** 2 MASKS

Mash 1 large (230g) ripe banana in a small bowl with ⅓ cup thick plain coconut yoghurt (or almond milk), ½ teaspoon vanilla extract and 1 tablespoon caster (superfine) sugar. To use, spread half the mask on clean face and neck; leave for 20 minutes. Rinse mask off with warm water then pat face dry. Place remaining mask in a small container or jar; cover the surface directly with plastic wrap and seal with a lid. Mask will keep in the fridge for up to 3 days.

PREP TIME 5 MINUTES **MAKES** 2 MASKS

Pulse ⅓ cup rolled oats, 2 tablespoons brown sugar (or demerara sugar) and 1 teaspoon ground cinnamon in a food processor until finely ground; tip into a bowl. Stir in 1 tablespoon melted coconut oil, followed by ½ cup water to form a thick paste. To use, spread half the mask on clean face and neck; leave for 20 minutes. Rinse mask off with warm water then pat face dry. Place remaining mask in a small container or jar; cover the surface directly with plastic wrap and seal with a lid. Mask will keep in the fridge for up to 3 days.

PREP + COOK TIME 50 MINUTES **SERVES** 4

MAC 'N' CHEESE

The 'cheese' sauce part of this recipe can be used layered with chargrilled eggplant for a baked dish.

- **500g (1lb) macaroni**
- **30g (1oz) vegan margarine**
- **¼ cup (40g) plain (all-purpose) flour**
- **1 teaspoon smoked paprika**
- **¼ teaspoon cayenne pepper**
- **¼ teaspoon garlic powder**
- **3 cups (750ml) macadamia milk**
- **225g (7oz) grated vegan mozzarella**
- **⅔ cup (55g) grated vegan parmesan (see page 17)**
- **1 tablespoon nutritional yeast flakes**

TEMPEH BACON BITS

- **300g (9½oz) tempeh**
- **2 tablespoons pure maple syrup**
- **2 teaspoons smoked paprika**
- **2 teaspoons tamari**
- **2 tablespoons olive oil**

1 Make tempeh bacon bits.

2 Cook macaroni in a large saucepan of boiling salted water for 8 minutes or until almost tender; drain. Return macaroni to pan.

3 Meanwhile, heat margarine in a medium saucepan over high heat. Add flour, smoked paprika, cayenne pepper and garlic powder; cook, stirring, for 2 minutes or until smooth and combined. Gradually add macadamia milk, stirring continuously, until mixture boils and thickens. Stir in vegan cheeses and nutritional yeast until cheeses melt; season to taste.

4 Stir hot cheese sauce into hot macaroni until combined. Spoon macaroni mixture into bowls. Serve topped with tempeh bacon bits.

tempeh bacon bits Crumble tempeh into tiny pieces. Place in two batches in a doubled piece of paper towel; squeeze tightly to remove excess moisture. Whisk maple syrup, smoked paprika and tamari in a small bowl. Heat olive oil in a non-stick frying pan over a medium heat; cook tempeh, stirring, for 8 minutes, breaking it up further with a wooden spoon, or until lightly browned and very dry. Add smoked paprika mixture; cook for a further 10 minutes or until dark, dry and crumbly. Drain on paper towel; season. Cool.

tip Tempeh bacon bits will keep refrigerated or up to 1 week. Scatter over baked sweet potatoes or salads for texture and flavour.

serving ideas Serve topped with finely chopped herbs such as chives or flat-leaf parsley.

PREP + COOK TIME 1 HOUR **SERVES** 4

Prep the spicy tomato sauce the day before to fast track the recipe for your movie night.

- **2 tablespoons flaxseed meal**
- **¼ cup (70g) dijon mustard**
- **2 tablespoons hot sauce (see tip)**
- **1⅔ cups (250g) plain (all-purpose) flour**
- **2 teaspoons onion powder**
- **2 teaspoons garlic powder**
- **2 teaspoons smoked paprika**
- **½ teaspoon cayenne pepper**
- **½ teaspoon ground white pepper**
- **1 medium cauliflower (1.5kg)**
- **vegetable oil, to deep-fry**

SPICY TOMATO SAUCE

- **2 tablespoons vegetable oil**
- **2 teaspoons brown mustard seeds**
- **1 medium onion (150g), chopped finely**
- **2 cloves garlic, sliced**
- **1 teaspoon ground ginger**
- **½ teaspoon cayenne pepper**
- **1 teaspoon freshly ground black pepper**
- **400g (12½oz) can crushed tomatoes**
- **⅓ cup (80ml) malt vinegar**
- **¼ cup (60ml) pure maple syrup**

1 Make spicy tomato sauce.

2 Combine flaxseed meal with ⅔ cup (160ml) water in a large bowl; stand for 5 minutes or until thickened. Add mustard and hot sauce; stir to combine. In a second large bowl, combine flour, powders, spices and white pepper; season with salt.

3 Cut cauliflower into 2.5cm (1in) florets.

4 Fill a large saucepan one-third full with oil; heat to 180°C/350°F (or until a cube of bread turns golden in 15 seconds). Add cauliflower to flaxseed mixture; stir to coat. Working in batches, toss cauliflower in flour mixture to coat. Carefully lower coated cauliflower into hot oil; fry for 2 minutes or until golden. Drain on paper towel. Season with salt.

5 Serve cauliflower with sauce.

spicy tomato sauce Heat oil in a saucepan over medium heat; cook mustard seeds for 30 seconds or until they pop. Add onion, garlic, spices and black pepper; cook, stirring, for 5 minutes or until onion softens. Add tomatoes, vinegar, maple syrup and ½ cup (125ml) water; bring to a simmer. Reduce heat to low; cook, for 25 minutes or until reduced and thickened. Cool.

tip Use whatever hot sauce you have on hand, such as sriracha or a mexican hot sauce.

serving idea Serve cauliflower popcorn with lemon wedges.

PREP + COOK TIME 45 MINUTES **SERVES** 4

GIANT BROWNIE SUNDAE

You can go the whole hog and add all the extras – sauce, ice-cream and toppings, or keep it simple.

- **1 cup (150g) plain (all-purpose) flour**
- **½ cup (110g) firmly packed brown sugar**
- **½ cup (110g) caster (superfine) sugar**
- **½ cup (65g) dutch-processed cocoa**
- **⅓ cup (80ml) vegetable oil**
- **1 teaspoon vanilla bean paste**
- **½ teaspoon sea salt flakes**
- **1 teaspoon baking powder**
- **75g (2½oz) vegan chocolate, chopped**
- **4 scoop chocolate soy ice-cream (400ml)**
- **15g (½oz) plain rectangular ice-cream wafers**
- **50g (1½oz) mini oreos**
- **8 maraschino cherries with stalks**
- **CHOCOLATE SAUCE**
- **¼ cup (60ml) pure maple syrup**
- **½ cup (65g) dutch-processed cocoa**
- **1 tablespoon coconut oil**
- **1 teaspoon vanilla bean paste**

1 Preheat oven to 180°C/350°F. Grease a 20cm (8in) cast iron frying pan or round cake pan or pie tin.

2 Place ¼ cup (35g) of the flour with ½ cup (125ml) water in a saucepan over medium heat; cook, whisking continuously, until mixture thickens. Transfer to a bowl; cool.

3 Stir sugars, cocoa, vegetable oil, vanilla paste and salt in a large bowl into a paste. Add the cooked flour mixture; stir until well combined. Stir in combined remaining sifted flour and baking powder, followed by chopped chocolate. (The mixture will be very thick.)

4 Press brownie mixture into pan; bake for 20 minutes or until a skewer inserted in the centre comes out clean.

5 Meanwhile, make chocolate sauce.

6 Top brownie with scoops of soy ice-cream, wafers, oreos and cherries; drizzle with chocolate sauce. Serve immediately.

chocolate sauce Place ingredients with ½ cup (125ml) water in a small saucepan; bring to a simmer, whisking occasionally until smooth, for 5 minutes. Cool. Sauce will thicken on cooling.

PREP + COOK TIME 30 MINUTES **SERVES** 2

SPICY VEGAN NACHOS

You could also make the nachos with purple hued beetroot corn chips and kidney beans if you like.

- **125g (4oz) corn chips**
- **½ cup (60g) vegan cheddar**
- **¼ teaspoon cumin seeds**
- **2 teaspoons olive oil**
- **1 small red onion (100g), chopped finely**
- **1 clove garlic, crushed**
- **2 teaspoons Tabasco**
- **2 tablespoons tomato paste**
- **400g (12½oz) can black beans, drained, rinsed**
- **1 medium tomato (150g), chopped finely**
- **1 fresh long red chilli, sliced thinly**
- **1 cup fresh coriander (cilantro) leaves**
- **1 tablespoon fresh lime juice**
- **1 medium avocado (250g), sliced**
- **lime wedges, to serve**

1 Preheat oven to 180°C/350°F. Line an oven tray with baking paper.

2 Place corn chips on oven tray, arranging them towards the outer edge; scatter over vegan cheddar. Bake for 8 minutes or until cheese melts and chips are heated through.

3 Meanwhile, heat a medium frying pan over medium heat, add cumin seeds stir for 2 minutes or until fragrant. Add olive oil, onion and garlic; cook, stirring, for 5 minutes or until onion is soft. Add Tabasco sauce and tomato paste; cook, stirring for 1 minute. Add beans and ⅓ cup (80ml) water; cook, stirring for 2 minutes or until thickened slightly. Lightly mash some of the beans in the pan with a fork or potato masher.

4 Combine tomato, chilli, coriander and lime juice in a small bowl. Season to taste.

5 Spoon black bean mixture over the corn chips. Top with avocado slices and tomato salsa, serve with lime wedges.

PREP + COOK TIME 45 MINUTES **SERVES** 4

Pick a bunch of rhubarb with stalks that are evenly sized, not too thick, and the reddest colour possible.

- **1 bunch rhubarb (500g), trimmed, cut into 3cm (1¼in) pieces**
- **500g (1lb) frozen strawberries**
- **1 teaspoon finely grated orange rind**
- **¼ cup (60ml) orange juice**
- **⅓ cup (50g) coconut sugar**
- **¾ cup (115g) plain (all-purpose) flour**
- **⅓ cup (30g) rolled oats**
- **¾ cup (90g) pecans, chopped**
- **½ cup (40g) shredded coconut**
- **1 teaspoon ground cinnamon**
- **¼ teaspoon ground nutmeg**
- **⅓ cup (75g) coconut oil, softened slightly**
- **icing (confectioners') sugar, to serve (optional)**

VANILLA BEAN CUSTARD

- **1 tablespoon arrowroot flour**
- **1½ cups (375ml) soy milk**
- **1 tablespoon caster (superfine) sugar**
- **½ teaspoon vanilla bean paste**
- **pinch of nutmeg**

1 Preheat oven to 180°C/350°F. Grease a 16cm x 23cm (6½in x 9¼in) rectangular 1.5 litre (6-cup) ovenproof dish. Place dish on an oven tray.

2 Place rhubarb, strawberries, orange rind, orange juice and half the coconut sugar in a medium saucepan over medium heat; cook, stirring occasionally, for 10 minutes or until rhubarb starts to soften and collapse. Transfer rhubarb mixture to ovenproof dish.

3 Meanwhile, for crumble, combine flour, remaining coconut sugar, the oats, pecans, shredded coconut and spices in a bowl. Using your fingertips, rub coconut oil into flour mixture until it forms a chunky crumble.

4 Top rhubarb mixture with crumble. Bake for 20 minutes or until crumble is golden and filling is cooked through.

5 Meanwhile, make vanilla bean custard.

6 Just before serving, dust crumble with icing sugar; serve with custard.

vanilla bean custard Stir arrowroot flour and 1 tablespoon water in a small bowl until smooth. Whisk soy milk and arrowroot mixture in a medium saucepan over medium heat. Bring to the boil, stirring continuously. Reduce heat to low, add sugar and vanilla paste; simmer for 5 minutes or until thickened slightly. Serve sprinkled with nutmeg.

food swaps In the crumble, you can use brown sugar instead of the coconut sugar. In the custard, you can use almond or coconut milk instead of the soy milk.

PREP + COOK TIME 1 HOUR 20 MINUTES **SERVES** 4

HARISSA EGGPLANT SKILLET LASAGNE

Serve this lasagne with a crisp green salad and garlic bread for an Italian feast.

- **100g (3oz) silver beet (swiss chard)**
- **600g (1¼lb) eggplants**
- **¼ cup (60ml) olive oil**
- **1 large onion (200g), chopped finely**
- **3 cloves garlic, crushed**
- **1 tablespoon harissa paste**
- **2 x 400g (12½oz) cans diced tomatoes**
- **1⅔ cups (410ml) vegetable stock**
- **¼ cup finely chopped fresh basil**
- **½ cup (80g) pine nuts**
- **2 tablespoons nutritional yeast flakes**
- **½ teaspoon sea salt flakes**
- **2 x 400g (12½oz) cans cannellini beans, drained, rinsed**
- **110g (3½oz) corrugated oven-ready dried lasagne sheets**
- **small basil leaves and extra olive oil, to serve**

1 Preheat oven to 200°C/400°F.

2 Remove stems from silver beet; chop finely, then tear leaves. Chop eggplant into 1cm (½in) pieces.

3 Heat oil in a large heavy-based, ovenproof frying pan over high heat (see tip). Add silver beet stems, eggplant, onion and 2 crushed cloves garlic; cook for 8 minutes, stirring occasionally, or until eggplant is golden and onion is soft. Add harissa; cook for 1 minute. Add tomatoes, 1 cup of the stock and the basil. Reduce heat; simmer for 5 minutes. Season to taste.

4 Meanwhile, process pine nuts, nutritional yeast and salt until finely chopped. Transfer to a small bowl.

5 Process beans, remaining garlic and remaining stock until smooth. Season to taste.

6 Break lasagne sheets in half. Press half the sheets into eggplant sauce, about halfway down the pan. Top sauce with silver beet leaves, pressing down into sauce. Top with remaining lasagne sheets, pressing down into sauce. Spread with cannellini bean mixture. Cover pan with foil.

7 Bake lasagne for 20 minutes. Remove foil; sprinkle with pine nut mixture. Bake, uncovered, for a further 20 minutes or until lasagne is bubbling and pine nuts are golden.

8 Serve lasagne topped with small basil leaves and drizzled with extra olive oil.

tip We used a frying pan with a top measurement of 28cm (11¼in) and a base measurement of 23cm (9¼in).

PREP + COOK TIME 50 MINUTES **SERVES** 4

CAULIFLOWER TACO MEAT

In winter months make the salsa from a ripe golden-fleshed pineapple, grapes or even crisp nashi pear.

- **600g (1¼lb) cauliflower, cut into florets**
- **1 cup (100g) walnuts**
- **2 tablespoons chopped chipotle chillies in adobo sauce**
- **2 teaspoons garlic powder**
- **½ cup (125ml) lime juice**
- **2 tablespoons extra virgin olive oil**
- **2 medium peaches (300g), chopped finely**
- **1 fresh long green chilli, seeded, cut into rounds**
- **½ small red onion (50g), chopped finely**
- **1 cup fresh coriander (cilantro) sprigs**
- **2 large avocados (640g)**
- **12 x 15cm (6in) white corn tortillas (300g)**

1 Preheat oven to 220°C/425°F. Line two oven trays with baking paper.

2 Process cauliflower, walnuts, chipotle and garlic powder until finely chopped. Transfer mixture to a large bowl; add ¼ cup of the lime juice and the oil, season. Mix well to combine. Spread mixture evenly on both trays. Roast for 30 minutes, stirring every 10 minutes, or until golden and crisp.

3 Meanwhile, combine peaches, fresh chilli, onion, half the coriander and 1 tablespoon of the remaining lime juice in a medium bowl; season to taste.

4 Cut avocados in half; remove stones. Mash avocado flesh with remaining lime juice in a medium bowl; season to taste.

5 Cook tortillas on a heated oiled grill pan (or frying pan) until warm and slightly charred. Serve cauliflower taco meat with tortillas, peach salsa, mashed avocado and remaining coriander.

Loaded hot chocolate

PERSIAN CHOCOLATE

PREP + COOK TIME 15 MINUTES **SERVES** 2

Pit and finely chop 8 medjool dates (160g). Place ¼ cup dutch-processed cocoa and ¼ teaspoon ground cardamom in a medium deep saucepan; slowly whisk in 2½ cups almond milk until well combined. Add chopped dates; slowly bring to the boil over low heat. Using a stick blender, blend on low speed until smooth. Add 1 teaspoon vanilla bean paste and 2 teaspoons rose water; stir until combined. (Taste the mixture and adjust the taste of the rose water as brands vary.) Pour into two large mugs. Top each mug with a handful of rose-flavoured pasmak (persian fairly floss), topped with 2 tablespoons slivered pistachios, 1 tablespoon cocoa nibs and dried rose petals, if you like.

SALTED WHITE CARAMEL

PREP + COOK TIME 15 MINUTES **SERVES** 2

Sprinkle ⅓ cup caster (superfine) sugar and ½ teaspoon crumbled salt flakes over the base of a medium heavy-based saucepan. Place pan over low-medium heat; cook without stirring until sugar dissolves and forms a golden caramel. Immediately add 20g (¾oz) coconut oil and ½ cup coconut cream; stir until caramel melts. Remove from heat; remove ¼ cup caramel mixture. Gradually stir 2 cups (500ml) almond milk and 2 teaspoons cornflour (cornstarch) into remaining caramel mixture in pan; cook, stirring, until mixture boils and thickens slightly. Pour into two large mugs. Top with a dollop of whipped coconut cream and reserved caramel. Scatter with caramel popcorn, if you like.

SPICED & SPIKED CHOCOLATE

PREP + COOK TIME 20 MINUTES (+ COOLING) **SERVES** 2

Place ½ cup water, ½ medium (240g) sliced orange, 2 whole star anise, ¼ cup firmly packed brown sugar and ⅓ cup spiced rum in a small saucepan; simmer gently over low heat until syrupy. Remove star anise and orange slices; discard. Stir in 150g (4½oz) finely chopped vegan dark chocolate until melted and smooth. Stir in 2 cups (500ml) almond milk; bring to a simmer, stirring occasionally. Pour into two large mugs. Top with a generous scoop of vegan vanilla ice-cream; dust with cocoa and sprinkle with finely grated orange rind.

THICK SPANISH CHOCOLATE

PREP + COOK TIME 15 MINUTES **SERVES** 2

Pour 2½ cups (625ml) almond milk into a medium saucepan with 2 cinnamon sticks. Remove 2 tablespoons milk from pan; stir together with 3 teaspoons cornflour (cornstarch) in a small cup to a smooth paste. Slowly bring milk almost to the boil over low heat so the milk has time to absorb the cinnamon flavour. Add 150g (4½oz) finely chopped vegan dark chocolate, cornflour mixture and a pinch of chilli powder; whisk until chocolate melts and mixture boils and thickens slightly. Discard cinnamon. Pour into two large mugs. Top with extra grated vegan dark chocolate, dust with cocoa and a pinch of ground chilli.

PREP + COOK TIME 1 HOUR **SERVES** 4

SPICED COCONUT RICE PUDDING WITH SAFFRON PEARS

For a twist on the saffron pears, replace the saffron with a small halved beetroot for pinkish pears.

- ¾ cup (150g) arborio rice
- 2 cups (500ml) almond and coconut milk
- ½ cup (125ml) coconut cream
- ¼ cup (55g) caster (superfine) sugar
- 2 fresh bay leaves
- 1 teaspoon sea salt flakes
- ⅓ cup (80ml) coconut cream, extra
- ⅓ cup (15g) flaked coconut, toasted

SAFFRON PEARS

- ½ cup (110g) caster (superfine) sugar
- ½ teaspoon saffron threads
- 2 star anise
- 3 pods cardamom, bruised
- 1 stick cinnamon
- 4 small corella pears (400g), peeled, halved, cored

1 Make saffron pears.

2 Place rice, milk, coconut cream and sugar in a deep non-stick medium saucepan over medium heat; cook, stirring, until mixture comes to a simmer. Stir in bay leaves. Reduce heat to low; cook for 25 minutes or until rice is just cooked. Stir in salt.

3 Divide pudding among bowls; top with extra coconut cream, a poached pear with syrup and flaked coconut.

saffron pears Stir sugar and 3 cups (750ml) water into a medium saucepan over medium heat until sugar dissolves. Bring to a simmer. Add spices and pears, making sure the pears are fully immersed in liquid. Reduce heat to low; cook pears for 20 minutes or until tender. Remove pears with a slotted spoon. Return poaching liquid to the heat; boil for 10 minutes or until liquid is a syrup consistency.

tips If the corella pears are very small, keep them whole and core from the base using a melon baller. If you have time, you can poach the pears a day ahead; this will intensify the flavour and colour.

food swap You can use ¼ teaspoon ground turmeric instead of the saffron, if you prefer.

PREP + COOK TIME 2 HOURS **SERVES** 4

DAIRY-FREE THYME POTATO BAKE

Dutch cream potatoes are a versatile waxy oval variety with a delicious buttery cream taste.

- **2 tablespoons vegan margarine**
- **2 tablespoons plain (all-purpose) flour**
- **½ teaspoon ground nutmeg**
- **1 litre (4 cups) almond milk**
- **2 tablespoons nutritional yeast flakes**
- **1.2kg (2½lb) dutch cream potatoes, peeled, sliced thinly**
- **½ cup (80g) blanched almonds, chopped coarsely**
- **¼ teaspoon sweet paprika**
- **2 tablespoons fresh thyme leaves**

1 Preheat oven to 180°C/350°F.

2 Heat margarine in a medium saucepan over medium heat until melted. Add flour and nutmeg; cook, stirring, for 2 minutes. Reduce heat to low; gradually add almond milk, stirring continuously until smooth. Stir in nutritional yeast. Increase heat to medium; cook, stirring, for 10 minutes or until sauce comes to a simmer. Remove from heat; season.

3 Grease a 3 litre (12-cup) ovenproof dish. Layer potatoes in dish. Pour white sauce over potatoes.

4 Cover dish with foil; bake for 40 minutes. Remove foil; bake, uncovered, for 40 minutes. Sprinkle with almonds and paprika. Return to oven; bake for a further 10 minutes or until potatoes are golden.

5 Scatter potato bake with thyme; stand for 10 minutes before serving.

food swaps You can use orange sweet potatoes instead of potatoes, however you will need to reduce the cooking time. If you like, add breadcrumbs with the almonds, for extra crunch on top.

PREP + COOK TIME 1 HOUR (+ STANDING) SERVES 4

PUMPKIN MAPLE WAFFLES WITH PECANS

Butternut pumpkin is the best variety to use for these waffles as it has dry dense flesh.

- 1⅓ cups (200g) white spelt flour
- 2 teaspoons baking powder
- ½ teaspoon sea salt flakes
- 2 teaspoons mixed spice
- ¾ cup (180ml) almond milk
- ¼ cup (60ml) olive oil
- ½ cup (120g) mashed cooked pumpkin (see tip)
- 2 tablespoons pure maple syrup, plus extra to serve
- 2 teaspoons vanilla extract
- cooking oil spray
- 4 scoops vanilla soy ice-cream
- ⅔ cup (80g) coarsely chopped pecans, roasted

1 Sift flour, baking powder, salt and mixed spice together into a large bowl. In a separate bowl, combine almond milk, oil, mashed pumpkin, maple syrup and vanilla until smooth.

2 Pour pumpkin mixture into flour mixture; stir until just combined but still with some lumps. Stand batter for 10 minutes.

3 Preheat waffle iron; spray with cooking oil. Gently stir batter. Pour ¼ cup of batter onto the centre of each square section of the waffle iron to just cover the base. Close the lid; cook for 3 minutes or until golden brown. Transfer to a wire rack. Repeat with remaining batter to make a total of 8 waffles.

4 Serve waffles topped with scoops of ice-cream, chopped pecans and extra maple syrup.

tip For mashed pumpkin, cook 180g (5½oz) peeled, seeded, chopped pumpkin with 1 tablespoon of water, in a microwave-safe bowl, covered with plastic wrap on HIGH (100%) for 8 minutes or until tender; mash. Alternatively, steam pumpkin in a steamer over a saucepan of simmering water until tender; mash.

PREP + COOK TIME 50 MINUTES (+ FREEZING) SERVES 6

CHOCOLATE SELF-SAUCING PUDDING WITH NO-CHURN ICE-CREAM

You will need to freeze the chopped bananas for the no-churn ice-cream a day ahead.

- 1 cup (150g) self-raising flour
- ⅓ cup (35g) dutch-processed cocoa, plus extra to dust
- 1 teaspoon ground cinnamon
- 1 teaspoon ground ginger
- ½ teaspoon ground nutmeg
- pinch of salt
- ¾ cup (165g) raw caster (superfine) sugar
- 1 tablespoon flaxseed meal
- 2 teaspoons vanilla bean paste
- ½ cup (125ml) almond milk
- 2 tablespoons almond butter
- ¾ cup (165g) firmly packed brown sugar

NO-CHURN ICE-CREAM

- 500g (1lb) bananas, chopped, frozen (see tips)
- 1 teaspoon vanilla bean paste
- 2 tablespoons pure maple syrup
- 2 tablespoons almond butter

1 Make no-churn ice-cream.

2 Preheat oven to 180°C/350°F. Grease a 1.75 litre (7 cup) round ovenproof dish; place on an oven tray.

3 Sift flour, half the cocoa, the spices and salt into a medium bowl. Stir in caster sugar and flaxseed meal. Whisk together vanilla paste, almond milk and almond butter in a small jug; pour over dry ingredients, stir until combined. Spoon into dish.

4 Combine brown sugar with remaining 2 tablespoons cocoa; sprinkle over the top of the chocolate batter. Slowly pour 1⅓ cups (330ml) boiling water over the back of a metal spoon to cover pudding.

5 Bake pudding for 35 minutes or until pudding bounces back when pressed gently in centre.

6 Serve pudding immediately dusted with extra cocoa and scoops of no-churn ice-cream.

no-churn ice-cream Process frozen banana until coarsely chopped. Add vanilla paste, maple syrup and almond butter; process until smooth. Spoon into a 2½ cup freezer proof container; freeze for 2 hours before scooping.

tips You will need approximately 2½ large (575g) bananas or 3 medium (600g) bananas. For accuracy, peel the bananas then weigh. For the best banana flavour use just ripe bananas.

serving ideas Top puddings with finely grated vegan chocolate and dried rose petals or buds.

PREP + COOK TIME 40 MINUTES SERVES 2

EGGPLANT DAN DAN NOODLES

This Sichuan-inspired dish is aromatic and fiery, inkeeping with food from this region of China.

- 1 tablespoon sambal oelek
- 1 tablespoon sesame oil
- 100ml vegetable oil
- 750g (1lb) eggplants, chopped finely
- 2 cloves garlic, crushed
- ¼ cup (60ml) kecap manis
- 270g (8½oz) dried udon noodles
- 2 fresh small red chillies, sliced thinly
- 2 tablespoons chopped fresh garlic chives

PEANUT SAUCE

- ½ teaspoon sichuan peppercorns
- ½ cup (240g) smooth peanut butter
- 2 tablespoons soy sauce
- 1 clove garlic, crushed

1 Combine sambal oelek, sesame oil and 2 tablespoons of the vegetable oil in a small bowl. Reserve chilli oil to serve.

2 Make peanut sauce.

3 Heat remaining ¼ cup vegetable oil in a large frying pan over medium high heat. Add eggplant, season with salt; cook, stirring occasionally, for 10 minutes or until softened and lightly golden. Add garlic; cook for 1 minute. Stir in kecap manis; cook for a further 2 minutes or until darkened and slightly caramelised. Remove from heat; cover to keep warm.

4 Cook noodles in a saucepan of boiling water for 8 minutes or until tender; drain.

5 Divide peanut sauce between bowls then top with the noodles. Serve topped with eggplant mixture, sliced chilli and garlic chives. Drizzle with reserved chilli oil.

peanut sauce Place peppercorns in a small frying pan; stir over medium heat for 3 minutes or until toasted and fragrant. Crush peppercorns with a mortar and pestle. Transfer to a bowl, add remaining ingredients and ⅔ cup (160ml) water; whisk until sauce is smooth.

PREP + COOK TIME 45 MINUTES (+ STANDING) **SERVES** 4

CAULIFLOWER & LEEK SOUP WITH CRISP SPROUT LEAVES

You will need to soak the cashews at least 2 hours ahead to soften them before starting the soup.

- **½ cup (75g) raw cashews**
- **¼ cup (60ml) extra virgin olive oil**
- **1 large onion (200g), chopped**
- **2 medium leeks (700g), sliced thickly**
- **2 cloves garlic, crushed**
- **1 medium cauliflower (1.5kg), trimmed, cut into florets**
- **1.5 litres (6 cups) vegetable stock**
- **1 tablespoon apple cider vinegar**
- **1 tablespoons finely chopped fresh thyme**
- **1 dried bay leaf**
- **1 teaspoon sea salt flakes**
- **½ teaspoon ground white pepper**
- **¼ cup (45g) pistachio dukkah**

CRISP SPROUT LEAVES

- **6 brussels sprouts (150g)**

1 Place cashews in a small bowl with enough cold water to cover. Stand for at least 2 hours. Drain. Rinse under cold water; drain well.

2 Heat 2 tablespoons of the oil in a large saucepan over medium heat; cook onion, stirring, for 3 minutes or until soft. Add leeks and garlic; cook for 5 minutes, stirring occasionally, or until leeks are soft.

3 Add cauliflower to pan; cook, stirring, for 1 minute. Add stock, vinegar, thyme, bay leaf, salt and pepper; bring to boil. Reduce heat; simmer, covered, for 15 minutes or until cauliflower is tender. Remove from the heat; discard bay leaf, then stir in drained cashews. Cool soup for 5 minutes.

4 Meanwhile, make crisp sprout leaves.

5 Blend soup in batches until as smooth as possible.

6 Reheat soup gently over medium heat; season to taste. Ladle soup into bowls; drizzle with remaining oil, then top with dukkah and sprout leaves.

crisp sprout leaves Preheat oven to 180°C/350°F. Line an oven tray with baking paper. Trim base of sprouts and separate leaves; spread evenly on the tray. Bake for 3 minutes or until golden brown and crisp.

tip You can sauté or roast the outer green leaves from the cauliflower in olive oil and serve on top of the soup instead of the sprout leaves.

PREP + COOK TIME 50 MINUTES SERVES 4

'STEAK' & MASH WITH HERBED GRAVY

Mushrooms have a savoury umami flavour and meaty texture making them a great meat substitute.

- ¼ cup (60ml) olive oil
- 2 tablespoons balsamic vinegar
- 4 cloves garlic, crushed
- 2 teaspoons smoked paprika
- 800g (1½lb) large portobello mushrooms, stalks removed

MASH

- 1kg (2lb) dutch cream potatoes, unpeeled, whole, scrubbed
- 1 cup (250ml) soy milk
- 40g (1½oz) vegan margarine

HERBED GRAVY

- ⅓ cup (50g) vegan gravy powder
- 1 cup (250ml) salt-reduced vegan beef-style stock
- 2 tablespoons brandy
- ¼ cup finely chopped fresh flat-leaf parsley

1 Place oil, balsamic, garlic and paprika in a screw-top jar. Season generously with salt and pepper; shake well to combine. Place mushrooms and balsamic mixture in a large zip-top bag; seal. Stand for 30 minutes.

2 Meanwhile, make mash then herbed gravy.

3 Heat a chargrill pan over high heat; line with baking paper. Cook mushrooms, covered with an upturned bowl or foil, for 2 minutes on each side until grill marks appear. Cut into thick slices.

4 Serve sliced mushrooms on mash, topped with herbed gravy and remaining parsley.

mash Place potatoes in a large saucepan with enough cold salted water to cover. Bring to the boil; cook for 30 minutes until tender. When potatoes are cool enough to handle, peel. Push potatoes through a ricer or a sieve into same cleaned saucepan. Return pan to a low heat, add soy milk and margarine; season to taste. Cook, stirring continuously, for 4 minutes or until milk and margarine are incorporated and mixture is smooth.

herbed gravy Whisk gravy powder, stock and brandy with 1 cup (250ml) water in a small saucepan over medium heat until mixture boils and thickens. Season to taste. Stir in half the parsley (reserve remaining parsley to serve).

tip Dutch cream potatoes will create a light fluffy mash; you could also use an all-rounder variety such as sebago.

serving idea Serve with green peas.

PREP + COOK TIME 55 MINUTES (+ STANDING) **SERVES** 4

SPICY NOT-KOTSU RAMEN

This is our playful and flavour-packed vegan take on tonkotsu, traditionally a pork-based dish.

- **¼ cup (60ml) olive oil**
- **2 teaspoons finely grated ginger**
- **6 cloves garlic, crushed**
- **4 green onions (scallions), sliced thinly, green tips shredded**
- **2 tablespoons spicy black beans in chilli oil**
- **2 tablespoons white (shiro) miso (see vegan hack)**
- **⅓ cup (80ml) mirin**
- **⅓ cup (80ml) soy sauce**
- **2 cups (500ml) soy milk**
- **2 corn cobs (500g)**
- **4 baby pak choy (240g), halved**
- **270g (8½oz) dried ramen noodles**
- **200g (6½oz) silken tofu, cubed**
- **2 tablespoons sesame seeds, toasted, crushed (see tip)**

DASHI

- **25g (¾oz) dried shiitake mushrooms**
- **40g (1½oz) dried kombu**

1 Make dashi.

2 Heat olive oil in a large saucepan over medium heat; cook ginger, garlic and green onion for 4 minutes or until softened. Add black beans and miso; cook, stirring, for 1 minute. Add mirin and soy sauce; bring to the boil.

3 Reduce heat to medium, add dashi and soy milk; cook for 5 minutes or until just below boiling point. Strain through a fine sieve; discard solids. Stir in reserved sliced shiitake.

4 Meanwhile, bring a large saucepan of water to the boil. Cook corn for 5 minutes or until tender; remove with tongs. Add pak choy to water; cook for 2 minutes or until tender, then remove with tongs. Add noodles to same water; cook for 5 minutes or until tender. Drain. Cut kernels from corn cobs.

5 Divide noodles and pak choy among bowls. Pour over hot broth. Top with corn kernels, shredded green onion and tofu. Serve sprinkled with sesame seeds.

dashi Place ingredients in a large saucepan with 1.5 litres (6 cups) cold tap water; slowly bring to the boil over low heat. Remove from heat; stand for 30 minutes for flavours to infuse. Strain liquid through a fine sieve into a large jug; slice shiitakes, reserving in a small bowl, and discard kombu.

tip To toast sesame seeds stir, continuously in small frying pan over medium heat until golden. Crush using a mortar and pestle.

vegan hack Check the ingredients listed on the miso pastes as some brands contain bonito (tuna) extract which is unsuitable for vegans.

PREP + COOK TIME 2 HOURS 15 MINUTES **MAKES** 4

FENNEL SHANK PIES

This playful twist on a lamb shank pie uses fennel instead, cooked in a hearty bean and tomato ragu.

- **4 large fennel bulbs (2.2kg)**
- **1 large onion (200g)**
- **2 large carrots (360g)**
- **¼ medium celeriac (celery root) (190g)**
- **2 tablespoons olive oil**
- **4 cloves garlic, sliced**
- **¼ cup (70g) tomato paste**
- **2 tablespoons finely chopped fresh lemon thyme**
- **2 tablespoons finely chopped fresh rosemary**
- **2 tablespoons vegan worcestershire sauce (see vegan hack)**
- **1 tablespoon dijon mustard**
- **½ cup (125ml) red wine**
- **2 cups (500ml) vegetable stock**
- **400g (12½oz) can diced tomatoes**
- **400g (12½oz) can chickpeas (garbanzo beans), drained, rinsed**

VEGAN PASTRY

- **1 tablespoon white chia seeds**
- **2 tablespoons soda water**
- **2 cups (320g) wholemeal plain (all-purpose) flour**
- **1 cup (150g) plain (all-purpose) flour**
- **¾ cup (180ml) extra virgin olive oil**
- **⅔ cup (160ml) soda water, extra**
- **¼ cup fresh thyme leaves**
- **1 teaspoon sea salt flakes**

1 Preheat oven to 190°C/375°F.

2 Trim top of fennel bulbs, leaving one of the centre stalks protruding. Reserve ¼ cup fennel fronds to serve. Using a paring knife, remove core from base of each fennel, by rotating the tip of the knife in a circular motion. Trim base slightly, so that fennel bulb sits level. Divide fennel among four 2½-cup (625ml) ceramic pie dishes. Roast for 40 minutes or until fennel is starting to soften.

3 Make vegan pastry.

4 Meanwhile, thinly slice onion. Peel carrot and celeriac; finely dice. Heat heat oil in a large heavy-based saucepan over medium heat. Add vegetables and garlic; cook, stirring occasionally, for 6 minutes or until they start to catch on the base of the pan and caramelise. Stir in tomato paste, herbs, sauce and mustard; cook for 2 minutes or until dry and fragrant. Add wine; cook, stirring, until reduced by half. Add stock, tomatoes and chickpeas; bring to the boil. Reduce heat to low; cook for 15 minutes or until thick. Season to taste.

5 Spoon vegetable mixture around fennel in dishes.

6 Roll a portion of pastry out on a lightly floured work surface until 4mm (¼in) thick. Cut a 2cm (¾in) hole in the centre of pastry. Carefully lift pastry over fennel bulb, positioning so the fennel stalk protrudes through the hole. Trim excess pastry. Press down on the edge to seal (alternatively, crimp pastry edges, using a finger and thumb). Cover fennel stalks with foil to prevent burning. Repeat with remaining pastry.

7 Bake pies for 40 minutes or until a knife inserted into fennel slides in easily and pastry is crisp.

vegan pastry Combine chia seeds and soda water in a small bowl, stand for 3 minutes. Process flours, oil, extra soda water, chia mixture, thyme and salt until mixture just comes together. Do not over mix. Transfer pastry to a clean work surface, bring together with your hands. Divide into four; wrap each portion in plastic wrap, refrigerate for 30 minutes.

do-ahead The pastry can be made a day ahead.

serving ideas Serve topped with extra salt flakes, finely grated lemon rind and reserved fennel fronds.

vegan hack Vegan worcestershire sauce is available from some major supermarkets and online; check the brand label carefully to ensure it does not contain anchovies. If unavailable, use tamari instead.

PREP + COOK TIME 2 HOURS **SERVES** 6

EGGPLANT & JACKFRUIT RAGU

Just like nonna used to make... except, of course, using jackfruit instead of the traditional meat.

- **4 medium red onions (680g), quartered**
- **3 cloves garlic**
- **⅓ cup (80ml) extra virgin olive oil**
- **1 large eggplant (500g), cut into 2cm (¾in) cubes**
- **2 x 565g (1¼lb) cans jackfruit in brine (see vegan hacks)**
- **¼ cup (60ml) balsamic vinegar**
- **1 tablespoon firmly packed brown sugar**
- **3 x 400g (12½oz) cans cherry tomatoes**
- **1 cup (250ml) vegetable stock**
- **1 cup fresh basil leaves**
- **500g (1lb) rigatoni pasta**
- **¼ cup (60ml) extra virgin olive oil, extra**
- **2 tablespoons pine nuts, toasted**

1 Process onion and garlic in a food processor until finely chopped.

2 Heat olive oil in a large heavy-based saucepan over high heat; cook eggplant, turning occasionally, for 5 minutes or until lightly golden. Add onion mixture; cook, stirring occasionally, for 6 minutes or until onion is soft.

3 Drain jackfruit; chop coarsely. Stir chopped jackfruit into onion mixture with vinegar, sugar, tomatoes and stock. Reduce heat to medium; cook, covered, stirring occasionally, for 1 hour or until ragu has thickened.

4 Add three-quarters of the basil. Reduce heat to low; cook ragu for a further 30 minutes.

5 Cook pasta in a large saucepan of boiling salted water for 8 minutes or until almost tender; drain. Add pasta to ragu with the extra olive oil; stir for a few minutes for pasta to absorb some of the ragu flavours.

6 Serve pasta and ragu topped with pine nuts and remaining basil.

vegan hacks Jackfruit is a South-East Asian fruit without a distinct taste and a fibrous texture much like meat. However, unlike meat it doesn't contain any protein; if you want to boost your protein intake, simply add a 400g can of drained and rinsed brown lentils to the ragu in step 3.

Easy nachos

SWEET POTATO & BLACK BEAN

PREP + COOK TIME 40 MINUTES **SERVES** 2

Preheat oven to 200°C/400°F. Place 400g (12½oz) thickly sliced sweet potatoes on a baking-paper-lined oven tray; season. Drizzle with 2 tablespoons olive oil; roast 20 minutes or until golden. Heat 2 tablespoons olive oil in a saucepan; cook 1 medium (150g) chopped onion for 10 minutes or until soft; reserve half. Add ½ teaspoon each ground cumin and coriander to pan; cook for 1 minute. Add 400g (12½oz) can crushed tomatoes and 400g (12½oz) can drained, rinsed black beans; cook 15 minutes. Place reserved onion in a small pan, stir in 2 teaspoons arrowroot, ½ teaspoon each powdered mustard and smoked paprika until grainy. Stir in 1 cup almond milk until smooth; boil, stirring, until thickened. Stir in 1 cup vegan cheddar. Divide sweet potato between shallow bowls; top with bean mixture, then drizzle with cheese sauce. Scatter with ½ cup coriander sprigs. Serve with lime wedges.

BRUSSELS SPROUTS & CORN

PREP + COOK TIME 45 MINUTES **SERVES** 2

Preheat oven to 240°C/475°F. Trim 400g (12½oz) brussels sprouts, then peel off leaves until too hard to do so; halve the heart. Place all sprouts on a baking-paper-lined oven tray; toss sprouts with 2 tablespoons olive oil, season. Roast for 15 minutes or until charred. Cut kernels from 2 corn cobs (500g). Heat 50g (1½oz) vegan margarine in a saucepan over medium heat; cook corn for 2 minutes. Reduce heat; cook, covered, stirring occasionally, for 15 minutes or until tender. Stir 2 teaspoons each combined plain (all-purpose) flour and water into corn until thickened. Reserve half the corn mixture. Using a stick blender, puree corn in pan; stir in reserved corn. Spread sprouts to edge of tray or platter; top with creamed corn, 200g (6½oz) chopped tomato, 1 chopped avocado and 1 finely sliced green onion (scallion).

Nachos doesn't always have to mean corn chips – vegetables can also be used in clever ways as a base for vegan toppings to be heaped onto.

BEETROOT NACHOS

PREP + COOK TIME 1½ HOURS **SERVES** 2

Preheat oven to 150°C/300°F. Line two oven trays with baking paper, then coat with cooking oil spray, sprinkle with sea salt flakes. Using a mandoline or V-slicer, cut 2 medium beetroot (700g) into paper-thin slices. Place in a single layer on trays. Spray with cooking oil; sprinkle with 1 teaspoon each ground cumin and smoked paprika. Bake for 1 hour. Top with ½ cup (50g) pepitas (pumpkin seed kernels); bake for a further 15 minutes or until crisp. Cool. Meanwhile, cook 1 medium (150g) chopped onion, 2 cloves garlic, 1 teaspoon each ground cumin and coriander in a medium frying pan with 2 tablespoons olive oil over medium heat for 8 minutes or until soft. Add a 400g (12½oz) can drained and rinsed kidney beans; stir until heated through. Serve beetroot chips with beans, topped with coriander and sliced cherry tomatoes, and vegan mayonnaise.

KALE CHIP & CHICKPEA

PREP + COOK TIME 30 MINUTES **SERVES** 2

Preheat oven to 180°C/350°F. Tear leaves from 250g (8oz) kale; divide between two baking-paper-lined oven trays. Coat well with olive oil spray, massage oil into kale. Bake for 15 minutes or until crisp. Cool. Process 1 medium (150g) onion, 2 cloves garlic, 1 teaspoon each ground cumin, coriander and sumac, 1 halved long fresh red chilli and ¼ cup olive oil until finely chopped. Cook onion mixture, stirring occasionally over medium heat, for 8 minutes. Add a 400g (12½oz) can drained and rinsed chickpeas and 1 cup vegetable stock; simmer for 10 minutes. Combine 1 chopped lebanese cucumber, 6 sliced radishes and 100g (3oz) halved cherry tomatoes in a small bowl. Serve kale chips with chickpea mixture, salad and ½ cup bought vegan garlic dip.

PREP + COOK TIME 3 HOURS 20 MINUTES **SERVES** 6

BEET WELLINGTON

It is important to buy beetroot that are equal in size with fresh green leaves attached.

- 6 large beetroots (beets) (1.2kg)
- ¼ cup (60ml) extra virgin olive oil
- 1½ tablespoons sherry vinegar
- 1½ tablespoons fresh thyme leaves
- 4 shallots, chopped finely
- 2 cups (200g) walnuts, roasted, chopped coarsely
- 2 tablespoons flaxseed meal
- 1 teaspoon ground nutmeg
- ⅓ cup (80ml) white wine
- 240g (7½oz) baby spinach leaves
- 3 sheets frozen puff pastry
- 1 tablespoon almond milk
- 1 teaspoon caster (superfine) sugar
- 1 teaspoon cracked black pepper

1 Preheat oven to 200°C/400°F. Line a small roasting pan and a large oven tray with baking paper.

2 Trim leaves from beetroots, wash and reserve leaves. Scrub beetroot; place in roasting pan. Combine 1 tablespoon each of the olive oil and vinegar with 1 tablespoon of the thyme leaves in a small bowl; season generously with salt and pepper. Brush beetroots all over with dressing. Cover pan with baking paper then foil; seal well.

3 Bake beetroot for 1 hour 20 minutes or until cooked through. Cool; peel, trim ends. Add 2 tablespoons water to hot roasting pan to release pan juices; strain into a small bowl, then stir in remaining vinegar; season to taste.

4 Meanwhile, heat remaining olive oil in a small frying pan over medium heat; cook shallots for 10 minutes. Add walnuts, flaxseed meal, nutmeg and remaining thyme. Stir in wine and ¼ cup (60ml) water; cook for 2 minutes. Season. Cool.

5 Blanch spinach in salted boiling water for 20 seconds; drain, refresh in iced water. Drain; squeeze out all the water you can. Pat dry with paper towel to help absorb excess moisture.

6 Cut 1 pastry sheet in half, then join each half to a whole pastry sheet; press along the join with your fingers to seal. Then, join the two extended pieces of pastry to each other by overlapping down a long side. You should end up with one large rectangle of pastry, approximately 36cm x 48cm (14¾in x 20in).

7 Spread cooled walnut mixture in the middle of the pastry, leaving an 8cm (3¼in) border on the long sides and 3cm (1¼in) border on the short sides. Press with your hands to compact mixture, then top with spinach unravelling it slightly so it sits flat and level. Place the beetroot upright on top, next to each other in a line. Trimming any excess pastry if necessary, roll pastry over beetroot to enclose filling. Tuck ends under and place on large oven tray.

8 Brush pastry generously with combined almond milk and sugar. Score the top and sprinkle with the pepper. Bake on the lowest shelf in the oven for 40 minutes, rotating the tray halfway through cooking.

9 Meanwhile, blanch reserved beetroot leaves in a saucepan of boiling water; drain. Toss leaves with a little olive oil; season.

10 Serve beet wellington sliced with beetroot leaves.

serving idea Serve with mashed potato and a horseradish cream; for horseradish cream, combine 1 teaspoon prepared horseradish with ⅓ cup vegan mayonnaise or vegan yoghurt.

PREP + COOK TIME 1 HOUR **SERVES** 4

JACKFRUIT RENDANG WITH SPELT FLATBREAD

You will find canned jackfruit in Asian grocers, check that the jackfruit is in brine not syrup.

- 4 dried red chillies (20g)
- 4 shallots, chopped
- 1 fresh long red chilli, chopped
- 4cm (1½in) fresh ginger, peeled, chopped coarsely
- 1 stalk lemon grass, white part only, chopped finely
- 4 cloves garlic, chopped
- 2 teaspoons grated fresh turmeric
- 2 tablespoons coconut oil
- 500g (1lb) jap pumpkin, peeled, cut into chunks
- 400ml coconut milk
- 2 x 565g (1¼lb) cans jackfruit in brine, drained, sliced
- ½ cup (40g) shredded coconut, toasted
- 1 tablespoon tamarind puree
- 1 lebanese cucumber (130g), cut into julienne
- 2 kaffir lime leaves, shredded finely

SPELT FLATBREAD

- 2 cups (260g) wholemeal spelt flour
- 1 teaspoon fine sea salt
- 2 tablespoons coconut oil, melted

1 Place dried chillies in a small heatproof bowl with enough boiling water to cover. Soak for 15 minutes. Drain; coarsely chop chillies.

2 Place chopped chillies in a food processor with shallots, fresh chilli, ginger, lemon grass, garlic and turmeric; process to a smooth paste.

3 Heat coconut oil in a large saucepan over medium heat; cook pumpkin, turning occasionally, for 5 minutes or until well browned. Remove from pan. Add curry paste; cook for 5 minutes or until starting to caramelise and almost all the liquid has evaporated.

4 Make spelt flatbread.

5 Stir coconut milk, 1½ cups (375ml) water, jackfruit and pumpkin into the sauce; simmer over medium heat for 15 minutes or until pumpkin is tender and sauce is very thick. Stir in half the toasted coconut and the tamarind puree. Season.

6 Divide rendang among bowls; top with remaining coconut, the cucumber and shredded kaffir leaves. Serve with flatbread for scooping.

spelt flatbread Mix flour, salt and ¾ cup (180ml) water in a large bowl into a soft dough. Knead lightly on a floured surface until smooth. Wrap dough in plastic wrap; stand for 15 minutes. Cut dough into 12 equal pieces; roll each piece on a lightly floured surface into a 2mm (⅛in) thick oval. Heat a large, heavy-based frying pan over high heat. Brush each flatbread lightly with coconut oil. Place half the flatbreads in the hot pan; cook for 2 minutes or until puffed and bubbled. Turn over; cook for a further 2 minutes or until well toasted. Repeat with remaining dough.

vegan hacks For a quick option, try using bottled rendang paste and 1 teaspoon ground turmeric for fresh curry paste. You can also serve the curry with steamed quinoa for added protein.

SUMMER VEGAN

PREP + COOK TIME 35 MINUTES SERVES 6 (MAKES 12)

CRUMBED ZUCCHINI SKEWERS WITH ROMESCO SAUCE

You will need 12 x 25cm (10in) long thin wooden skewers for this recipe.

- 6 medium zucchini (720g), halved crossways (see tips)
- ½ cup (125ml) extra virgin olive oil
- ¾ cup (105g) gluten-free breadcrumbs (see tips)
- ½ cup (70g) vegan parmesan (see page 17)

ROMESCO SAUCE

- 260g (8½oz) jar roasted red capsicums (bell peppers), drained
- 1 clove garlic, crushed
- ½ cup (80g) blanched almonds, roasted
- 2 tablespoons sherry vinegar
- 1 teaspoon smoked paprika
- 2 tablespoons chopped fresh flat-leaf parsley
- ⅓ cup (80ml) extra virgin olive oil

1 Preheat oven to 200°C/400°F. Line an oven tray with baking paper.

2 Make romesco sauce.

3 Insert a wooden skewer lengthways through the centre of each zucchini half. Place a zucchini half on a chopping board. Hold the skewer with one hand, with the other hand, cut into the zucchini 2cm (¾in) from the top at a 45 degree angle, down to the skewer, continue cutting and rotating the skewer simultaneously maintaining the cut into the top end at a 45 degree angle, roll the zucchini away from you while continuing to slice around it in one continuous motion. Try to keep your knife against the skewer as a guide to create the spiral, always cutting lower than the previous slice so it stays together. Spread spirals along skewer. Repeat with remaining skewers and zucchini halves.

4 Place zucchini skewers on oven tray. Brush oil evenly over zucchini spirals and into each cut. Coat spirals in combined crumbs and vegan parmesan, ensuring the coating covers the inside cut surface of the spirals. Season.

5 Bake for 15 minutes or until golden brown and zucchini is tender.

6 Serve zucchini skewers with romesco sauce.

romesco sauce Process ingredients until smooth; season.

tips When buying the zucchini, make sure to choose ones that are as straight as possible; this will make it easier to create the spiral cut. We used Orgran brand crispi crumbs, which are gluten-free breadcrumbs; available from supermarkets.

MOJO

PREP + COOK TIME 20 MINUTES (+ FREEZING) **MAKES** 12

FRUITY VEGAN SOFT SERVES

You will need to prepare the fruit purees, then freeze for at least 4 hours before piping to serve.

AVOCADO & LIME

- **3 large avocados (960g), halved, stone removed, chopped**
- **⅓ cup (80ml) fresh lime juice**
- **⅔ cup (105g) icing (confectioners') sugar, sifted**
- **1 teaspoon finely grated lime rind**

BANANA & RASPBERRY

- **200g (6oz) frozen raspberries**
- **800g (1½lb) over-ripe bananas, peeled, chopped coarsely**

MANGO & PASSSIONFRUIT

- **900g (1¾lb) frozen diced mango**
- **¼ cup passionfruit pulp**

1 To make avocado and lime soft serve, process avocado, lime juice and sugar until very smooth. Pour into a large zip-lock bag; seal. Freeze flat for 4 hours or until puree is solid. Break frozen puree into chunks and process until smooth. Spoon soft serve into a piping bag fitted with a star tube. Immediately pipe mixture into cups or ice-cream cones; sprinkle with lime rind to serve. (Makes 2½ cups.)

2 To make banana and raspberry soft serve, place frozen raspberries in a food processor; pulse quickly and briefly to roughly crumble. Remove a quarter; reserve in the freezer until ready to serve. Add banana to the remaining raspberries, process until very smooth. Pour into a large zip-lock bag; seal. Freeze flat for 4 hours or until puree is solid. Break frozen puree into chunks and process until smooth. Spoon soft serve into a piping bag fitted with a star tube. Immediately pipe mixture into cups or ice-cream cones; sprinkle with frozen crumbled raspberries to serve. (Makes 2½ cups.)

3 To make mango and passionfruit soft serve, process mango until very smooth. Add half the passionfruit; pulse until well combined. Pour into a large zip-lock bag; seal. Freeze flat for 4 hours or until puree is solid. Break frozen puree into chunks and process until smooth. Spoon soft serve into a piping bag fitted with a star tube. Immediately pipe mixture into small cups or ice-cream cones. Drizzle with remaining passionfruit to serve. (Makes 3½ cups.)

tips To pipe the soft serves, you will need three disposable piping bags and three star tubes. The soft serve can be stored in the piping bags in the freezer for up to 2 hours before becoming too firm to pipe.

PREP + COOK TIME 1 HOUR 15 MINUTES (+ REFRIGERATION) **SERVES** 2

WATERMELON 'TUNA' POKE BOWL

Watermelon is cleverly transformed here to take the place of sashimi tuna. Start the day ahead.

- ¼ cup (60ml) extra virgin olive oil
- 600g (1¼lb) seedless watermelon, cut into 2cm (¾in) pieces
- ¼ cup (60ml) rice wine vinegar
- 2 radishes (70g), sliced thinly
- 1 lebanese cucumber (130g), sliced thinly
- 2 tablespoons rice wine vinegar, extra
- 250g (8oz) packet microwave brown rice
- 2 cups (160g) shredded green cabbage
- 1 small avocado (200g), sliced thinly
- 1 cup snow pea tendrils
- 1 green onion (scallion), sliced thinly
- 2 tablespoons wasabi peas, chopped coarsely

GINGER HOISIN DRESSING

- 2 tablespoons hoisin sauce
- ¼ cup (60ml) lime juice
- 2 tablespoons extra virgin olive oil
- 1 teaspoon grated fresh ginger
- 1 fresh small red chilli, chopped finely

1 Preheat oven to 200°C/400°F.

2 Drizzle 1½ tablespoons of the oil over the base of an ovenproof dish. Spread watermelon out in a single layer over base of dish. Drizzle with remaining oil. Roast for 30 minutes. Drizzle with vinegar; roast for a further 20 minutes. Cool watermelon in dish, then transfer to a medium bowl with the pan juices. Cover; refrigerate until cool or overnight.

3 Combine radish, cucumber and extra vinegar in a medium glass or stainless steel bowl; season. Stand for 5 minutes; drain.

4 Reheat rice according to packet instructions.

5 Make ginger hoisin dressing.

6 Drain watermelon. Place rice in bowls; arrange cabbage, pickled vegetables, watermelon, avocado and snow pea tendrils on top. Drizzle with dressing, then top with green onion and wasabi peas.

ginger hoisin dressing Combine ingredients in a small bowl; season to taste.

tips Snow pea tendrils are the tender part of the snow pea vine, they are packed like rocket leaves in greengrocers. You could also use snow pea shoots or bean sprouts.

serving idea You can top the bowls with shredded nori sheets for a more oceany flavour.

PREP + COOK TIME 35 MINUTES (+ REFRIGERATION) **SERVES** 2

MEXICAN BARBECUE FEAST FOR TWO

This is a feast for two very hungry people; enjoy any leftovers or halve the tomatoes and asparagus.

- 250g (8oz) tempeh
- ¼ cup (60ml) lime juice
- 1 tablespoon olive oil
- 2 teaspoons pure maple syrup
- 2 teaspoons cumin
- ¼ teaspoon cayenne pepper
- 1 medium avocado (250g), halved, stone removed
- 1 bunch asparagus (170g), trimmed
- 375g (12oz) small truss tomatoes
- 2 tablespoons vegan mayonnaise (just like mayo, see page 17)
- ½ teaspoon smoked paprika
- 2 corn cobs (500g), in the husk
- 4 mini white corn tortillas (100g)
- 1 lime (65g), cut into wedges

PEPITA DRESSING

- ½ cup (100g) pepitas (pumpkin seed kernels), toasted
- ⅓ cup (80ml) lime juice
- ½ cup (125ml) extra virgin olive oil
- 1 small clove garlic, crushed
- 2 tablespoons finely chopped fresh coriander (cilantro)

1 Cut tempeh in half crossways, then cut each half horizontally to make 4 thin 'steaks'. Combine lime juice, oil, maple syrup, cumin and cayenne pepper in a shallow dish. Add tempeh steaks; turn to coat in marinade. Cover; refrigerate for 1 hour.

2 Make pepita dressing.

3 Heat an oiled barbecue (or large grill plate) over high heat. Barbecue avocado halves, cut-side down, for 2 minutes or until grill marks appear. Barbecue asparagus, turning occasionally, for 4 minutes or until just tender. Barbecue tomatoes, turning occasionally, for 4 minutes or until softened and starting to blister.

4 Barbecue tempeh for 2 minutes on each side or until heated through and grill marks appear.

5 Combine mayonnaise and ¼ teaspoon of the paprika in a small bowl. Peel back husks from corn cobs; barbecue corn, turning occasionally, for 8 minutes or until kernels are tender and charred. Dollop hot cobs with mayonnaise mixture; sprinkle with remaining paprika.

6 Arrange all barbecued ingredients on a large platter or board with tortillas and lime wedges; serve with pepita dressing.

pepita dressing Process all the ingredients until it forms a chunky pesto-like consistency. Season.

tip If your barbecue is large enough, cook all the ingredients at once.

PREP + COOK TIME 45 MINUTES **SERVES** 2

CHARRED TOFU WITH CHIMICHURRI & RADISH SLAW

Chimichurri is an Argentinian herb sauce that's delicious with vegies especially barbecued ones.

- ¼ small red cabbage (200g), shredded finely
- 4 red radishes (140g), sliced very thinly
- 2 tablespoons apple cider vinegar
- ½ teaspoon caraway seeds, toasted
- 300g (9½oz) firm tofu
- 2 tablespoons extra virgin olive oil
- ½ teaspoon smoked paprika
- ½ teaspoon garlic powder
- ½ teaspoon onion powder
- 1 lime (65g), halved
- 4 greek yiros wraps (380g)
- ½ cup (60g) vegan garlic dip

CHIMICHURRI

- 1 cup fresh mint leaves
- 1 cup fresh coriander (cilantro) leaves
- 1 clove garlic, crushed
- 1 fresh long red chilli, seeded, chopped finely
- 1 teaspoon grated fresh ginger
- ⅓ cup (80ml) extra virgin olive oil
- 2 tablespoons apple cider vinegar

1 Place cabbage, radishes, vinegar and caraway seeds in a medium bowl, season with salt and pepper; toss gently to combine.

2 Make chimichurri.

3 Slice tofu into 1cm (½in) thick slices. Brush both sides with olive oil. Combine paprika with garlic and onion powders; sprinkle mixture on both sides of the tofu.

4 Preheat a chargrill pan (or frying pan) over medium-high heat. Cook tofu slices for 1½ minutes each side or until slightly charred; transfer to a tray. Chargrill lime halves, cut-side down, for 1 minute or until caramelised.

5 Serve tofu on radish slaw, topped with garlic dip and chimichurri. Serve with wraps and lime halves.

chimichurri Finely chop mint and coriander. Combine herbs with remaining ingredients in a bowl; season to taste.

PREP + COOK TIME 30 MINUTES (+ REFRIGERATION) **SERVES** 4

CARDAMOM FRUIT SALAD WITH COCONUT LABNE

You will need to drain the yoghurt for the labne at least 8-24 hours ahead of serving.

- **500g (1lb) coconut yoghurt (see tips)**
- **1 teaspoon vanilla bean paste**
- **½ teaspoon sea salt flakes, crumbled**
- **½ cup (125ml) pure maple syrup**
- **1 teaspoon ground cardamom**
- **¼ cup (60ml) strained orange juice**
- **250g (8oz) pineapple, peeled, cored, sliced into wedges**
- **cooking oil spray**
- **1 medium blood orange (340g), peeled, sliced (see tips)**
- **¼ medium rockmelon (425g), sliced**
- **1 dragon fruit (500g), peeled, sliced**
- **½ cup (25g) flaked coconut, toasted**
- **2 tablespoons fresh mint leaves**
- **1 lime (65g), cut into wedges**

1 Combine yoghurt, vanilla paste and salt in a medium bowl. Place a sieve over a small bowl; line with muslin. Spoon yoghurt mixture into muslin; gather into a ball, secure with string or an elastic band. Refrigerate for 8 hours or overnight.

2 Combine maple syrup and cardamom in a small saucepan; bring to the boil over medium-high heat. Reduce heat; simmer for 3 minutes or until syrupy. Stir in orange juice. Cool.

3 Preheat a chargrill pan (or frying pan) over high heat. Spray pineapple wedges with cooking oil; cook pienapple on all sides for 2 minutes or until grill marks appear.

4 Remove yoghurt from muslin; place into a small bowl.

5 Arrange pineapple, blood orange, rockmelon and dragon fruit on a platter; drizzle with syrup mixture. Top with spoonfuls of labne, toasted coconut and mint leaves. Serve with lime wedges.

tips We used a thick unsweetened coconut yoghurt (Coyo). The season for blood oranges starts late winter and runs until mid-spring. Substitute with oranges or pink grapefruit.

PREP + COOK TIME 45 MINUTES (+ REFRIGERATION) **SERVES** 4

BLACK RICE NOODLE SALAD WITH MANGO & TEMPEH

Black rice noodles get their colour from anthocyanin a dark blue flavonoid antioxidant.

- 2 tablespoons tamari
- 1 tablespoon rice wine vinegar
- 1 tablespoon pure maple syrup
- 2 teaspoons grated fresh ginger
- 250g (8oz) tempeh, cut into 5mm (¼in) thick slices
- ⅓ cup (80ml) lime juice
- ¼ cup (60ml) extra virgin olive oil
- 2 tablespoons tamari
- 2 teaspoons coconut sugar
- 1 fresh long red chilli, sliced finely
- 1 teaspoon sesame oil
- 250g (8oz) packet black rice noodles (see vegan hacks)
- 1 medium mango (430g), peeled, sliced
- 1 lebanese cucumber (130g), peeled into strips
- ½ cup (75g) roasted cashews, chopped coarsely
- ½ cup fresh thai basil leaves
- lime wedges, to serve

1 Combine tamari, vinegar, maple syrup and ginger in a shallow bowl or tray. Add tempeh; turn to coat well. Cover with plastic wrap; refrigerate for 1 hour.

2 Combine lime juice, 2 tablespoons of the olive oil, the tamari, coconut sugar, chilli and sesame oil in a small bowl.

3 Cook noodles in a saucepan of boiling water for 5 minutes or until softened. Drain. Rinse under cold running water; drain. Transfer to a large bowl.

4 Heat remaining olive oil in a medium frying pan over a medium-high heat; cook tempeh and marinade for 1 minute on each side or until browned lightly.

5 Add lime dressing and tempeh to noodles with mango, cucumber, cashews and basil; toss gently to coat. Serve with lime wedges.

vegan hacks Black rice noodes contain superior amounds of dietary fibre, protein and antioxidants compared to ordinary white rice noodles.

PREP + COOK TIME 45 MINUTES **SERVES** 4

AMERICAN BARBECUE BOX

Serve the components in a take away box for each person to fill their bread rolls as they wish.

- 2 x 565g (1¼lb) cans jackfruit in water, drained, rinsed
- 2 tablespoons olive oil
- 1 large onion (200g), sliced thinly
- 3 cloves garlic, crushed
- 1 teaspoon ground cumin
- ½ teaspoon chilli powder
- 1 teaspoon smoked paprika
- 330ml can Dr Pepper
- 1 cup (250ml) vegan beef-style stock
- ½ cup (140g) smokey barbecue sauce
- 425g (13½oz) packet corn cobbettes (see tips)
- 4 small soft white bread rolls (120g)
- 8 whole dill pickles (170g)

COLESLAW

- 2 cups (160g) finely shredded green cabbage
- 1 small carrot (70g), cut into matchsticks
- 1 small green-skinned apple (130g), cut into matchsticks
- 2 tablespoons apple cider vinegar
- ⅓ cup (100g) vegan mayonnaise (just like mayo, see page 17)

1 Using a small knife, cut the core from the jackfruit pieces; discard. Remove and discard seeds.

2 Heat oil in a large non-stick frying pan over medium heat; cook onion, stirring, for 4 minutes or until softened. Add garlic; cook for 1 minute.

3 Stir in cumin, chilli powder and paprika. Add jackfruit, Dr Pepper, stock and barbecue sauce. Increase heat to high; cook for 15 minutes or until mixture is thick and sticky. Shred jackfruit into meat-like strands, using two forks; stir through sauce until well coated. Season to taste.

4 Meanwhile, make colelsaw.

5 Preheat a barbecue or chargrill pan to medium. Cook corn, turning frequently, for 6 minutes or until tender. Split rolls in half, place, cut-side down, on barbecue for 1 minute or until grill marks appear.

6 Serve pulled 'pork' with coleslaw, corn cobettes, pickles and bread rolls.

coleslaw Place cabbage, carrot and apple in a large bowl with vinegar; toss to combine. Stand for 5 minutes to soften. Stir in mayonnaise; season to taste.

tips Use a julienne peeler to finely shred carrot if available. Corn cobbettes, are small pieces of cut corn cob; about a quarter to one third the size of a full cob of corn.

Body beauty

BROWN SUGAR SCRUB

PREP TIME 10 MINUTES **MAKES** 1 CUP

Place a heatproof bowl over a saucepan of boiling water; take off the heat. Add 2 tablespoons coconut oil, 2 tablespoons rice bran oil and 1 tablespoon rice malt syrup; stir until ingredients are combined. Remove bowl from pan; stand until cool to the touch. Stir in ½ cup each brown sugar and white (granulated) sugar. You can stop there, or to fortify the scrub, add 1 vitamin E oil capsule, 1 teaspoon jojoba oil and 5 drops lavender essential oil (or other favourite essential oil). Spoon into a jar. To use, remove desired amount of scrub from jar with a spoon before stepping into the shower. Massage scrub onto wet skin in a circular motion. Rinse off.

BUFF & GLOW COFFEE SCRUB

PREP TIME 10 MINUTES **MAKES** 1⅓ CUPS

Place a heatproof bowl over a saucepan of boiling water; take off the heat. Add 2 tablespoons coconut oil and 2 tablespoons rice bran oil; stir until ingredients are combined. Remove bowl from pan; stand until cool to the touch. Add 1 cup white (granulated) sugar, ¼ cup ground coffee beans and 1 teaspoon vanilla extract. You can stop there, or to fortify the scrub, add 2 vitamin E oil capsules and 5 drops pink grapefruit essential oil (or other favourite essential oil). Spoon into a jar. To use, remove desired amount of the scrub from jar with a spoon before stepping into the shower. Massage scrub onto wet skin in a circular motion. Rinse off.

SUMMER HAIR REVIVER

PREP TIME 5 MINUTES **MAKES** ENOUGH FOR 1 USE

Salt, sun and chlorine can all take their toll on your locks. Apply this mask fortnightly over summer to add back shine and softness.

Part One: Process ½ avocado and 1 small banana until smooth. Add 1 teaspoon rice bran syrup and 1 tablespoon extra virgin olive oil; process until combined. Spoon into a small bowl. Spread mask over hair. Pile hair ontop of your head and wrap your hair in plastic wrap. Leave for 15 minutes for mixture to soak in. Rinse well.

Part Two: Fill a jug with 1 teaspoon apple cider vinegar and warm water; pour through hair to remove any excess mask.

SKIN PAMPERING WHIP

PREP TIME 10 MINUTES (+ STANDING) **MAKES** 1¼ CUPS

Place a heatproof bowl over a saucepan of boiling water; take pan with bowl off the heat. Add 150g (4½oz) cocoa butter; stir until melted. Remove bowl from heat, stir in 2 tablespoons avocado oil or sweet almond oil and 1 teaspoon arrowroot powder. Place the bowl in the fridge for 20 minutes or until oil has firmed but not solidified. Add 10 drops of your favourite essential oil (try lavender for oily skin, cedarwood or rose for dry skin and bergamont for combination skin). Blend in a high-powered blender until a creamy consistency. Spoon into a small clean jar. To use, remove a small amount of whip from the jar with a teaspoon; massage onto parched skin, in particular dry legs, feet and elbows.

PREP + COOK TIME 40 MINUTES (+ FREEZING) **SERVES** 8

FROZEN NO-BAKE BLUEBERRY & LIME MERINGUE SLAB

To brown the meringue, you will need a kitchen blowtorch, available from kitchen or hardware stores.

- **1 cup (90g) rolled oats**
- **1 cup (160g) natural almonds, roasted**
- **¾ cup (175g) fresh medjool dates**
- **¼ cup (60ml) extra virgin olive oil**
- **1 tablespoon pure maple syrup**
- **½ teaspoon sea salt flakes**
- **2 cups (300g) frozen blueberries**
- **300g (9½oz) silken tofu**
- **270ml can coconut cream**
- **½ cup (120g) barley malt syrup**
- **1 teaspoon vanilla extract**
- **2 limes (130g), rind cut into strips (see tips), juiced**

ITALIAN MERINGUE

- **1 cup (220g) caster (superfine) sugar**
- **⅓ cup (80ml) water**
- **400g (12½oz) can chickpeas (garbanzo beans), unopened**
- **2 teaspoons cream of tartar**

1 Line a 8cm (3¼in) deep, 12cm x 25cm (4¾in x 9¼in) loaf pan with two layers of baking paper, extending the papers 5cm (2in) over the two long sides.

2 Process oats, almonds, dates, oil, maple syrup and salt until coarsely combined and sticking together well. Press mixture evenly and firmly onto base of lined pan.

3 Place blueberries, tofu, coconut cream, barley malt syrup, vanilla and ¼ cup lime juice in a food processor; process until smooth. Pour into loaf pan; freeze for 2 hours or until set.

4 Make italian meringue.

5 Spoon italian meringue over blueberry layer; using the back of a spoon, swirl meringue to form peaks. Using a blowtorch, lightly brown the meringue (see tips); return to the freezer for 30 minutes or until ready to serve.

6 Serve topped with lime rind and extra fresh blueberries, if you like.

italian meringue Place sugar and the water in a small saucepan, stir gently. Place pan over medium heat; cook without stirring, for 15 minutes or until syrup reaches 118°C/244°F on a cooking thermometer. Meanwhile, strain chickpeas through a sieve over a small bowl; you should have ¾ cup (180ml) chickpea liquid (aquafaba). Reserve chickpeas for another use (see tips). Place aquafaba in the bowl of an electric mixer, whisk on high speed until tripled in volume; whisk in cream of tartar. When sugar syrup reaches 120°C/250°F, slowly pour into meringue mixture. Increase speed to maximum; whisk for a further 3 minutes or until the bowl feels room temperature when touched.

tips Use the chickpeas to make the cauliflower hummus on page 63, or the carrot and turmeric hummus on page 279. If you don't have a kitchen blowtorch, place the dessert under a hot grill (broiler) for 30 seconds or until meringue is lightly browned.

PREP + COOK TIME 30 MINUTES **SERVES** 4

GREEK SALAD WITH NUT FETTA

We used green zebra tomatoes, a heirloom variety of green tomatoes, but you can use any type.

- 1 tablespoon extra virgin olive oil
- 1 clove garlic, crushed
- 400g (12½oz) can butter beans, drained, rinsed
- 1 teaspoon dried chilli flakes
- 2 baby cos (romaine) lettuce (400g), trimmed, quartered
- 500g (1lb) mixed green heirloom tomatoes, sliced
- 200g (6½oz) baby cucumbers, sliced lengthways, chopped
- 1 medium yellow capsicum (bell pepper) (200g), seeded, sliced
- ½ cup (80g) pitted kalamata olives, torn
- 120g (4oz) marinated almond or macadamia fetta
- ¼ cup fresh oregano leaves

OREGANO DRESSING

- ¼ cup (60ml) extra virgin olive oil
- 1 tablespoon white wine vinegar
- 2 tablespoons lemon juice
- 1 small clove garlic, crushed
- 1 teaspoon dried oregano
- ½ teaspoon caster (superfine) sugar

1 Make oregano dressing.

2 Heat oil in a medium frying pan over medium-high heat; cook garlic and beans for 5 minutes, stirring occasionally, or until beans are starting to brown and crisp. Remove from heat; sprinkle with chilli flakes, cool in pan.

3 Arrange lettuce, bean mixture, tomatoes, cucumber and capsicum on a large platter or individual plates; top with olives and fetta.

4 Drizzle salad with dressing and scatter with oregano leaves.

oregano dressing Place ingredients in a screw-top jar; shake very well. Season to taste.

WEEKEND
VEGAN

ROAST VEGETABLE & PESTO LASAGNE

Serve the lasagne with a rocket, shaved fennel and pear salad for an Italian feast.

- 2 large red capsicums (bell peppers) (700g)
- ¼ cup (60ml) olive oil
- 4 large zucchini (600g), sliced thinly lengthways
- 2 medium eggplant (600g), sliced thinly lengthways
- 6 fresh lasagne sheets (300g)
- 150g (4½oz) baby spinach leaves
- ½ cup (40g) finely grated vegan cheddar

BÉCHAMEL SAUCE

- 60g (2oz) vegan margarine
- ¼ cup (35g) plain (all-purpose) flour
- 3 cups (750ml) almond milk
- ½ cup (40g) finely grated vegan cheddar

PESTO

- ⅓ cup (50g) pine nuts, toasted
- 2 cloves garlic, quartered
- 1½ cups firmly packed fresh basil leaves
- ½ cup (125ml) olive oil

1 Preheat oven to 200°C/400°F. Oil a deep 3-litre (12-cup) ovenproof dish.

2 Quarter capsicums; discard seeds and membranes, then slice thickly.

3 Heat a little of the olive oil in a large frying pan over medium heat. In separate batches, cook capsicum, zucchini then eggplant, adding more of the oil before each batch as necessary until vegetables are browned on both sides. Keep vegetables separate. Season.

4 Make béchamel sauce, then pesto.

5 Layer zucchini in dish; top with one-third of the pesto, two lasagne sheets and one-third of the béchamel sauce. Repeat layering, replacing vegetable layer with eggplant, then capsicum and 100g (3oz) of the spinach. Cover dish with foil.

6 Bake lasagne for 40 minutes. Remove foil; sprinkle with vegan cheddar. Bake, uncovered, for a further 15 minutes or until browned. Stand for 10 minutes before serving, topped with remaining spinach leaves.

béchamel sauce Melt margarine in a medium saucepan over medium heat, add flour; cook, stirring, until mixture bubbles. Gradually add almond milk, stirring until mixture boils and thickens. Remove from heat; stir in vegan cheddar. Season to taste.

pesto Process pine nuts, garlic and basil until finely chopped. With motor operating, gradually add oil in a thin, steady stream until combined. Season to taste.

vegan hacks For a short-cut use ready-made vegan pesto and char-grilled deli vegetables.

PREP + COOK TIME 45 MINUTES (+ OVERNIGHT REFRIGERATION) **MAKES** 12

OVERNIGHT JASMINE TEA & LEMON CURD SCROLLS

You will need to start this recipe the day before, for the dough to rise slowly in the fridge overnight.

- 3 green tea with jasmine tea bags
- 1 teaspoon finely grated lemon rind
- 2 tablespoons pure maple syrup
- 3 cups (450g) bread flour
- 1 teaspoon (4g) dried yeast
- 1½ teaspoons sea salt flakes
- 1 teaspoon ground cardamom
- finely grated lemon rind and chopped pistachios, extra, to serve (optional)

NUT FILLING

- ½ cup (70g) pistachios, chopped coarsely
- ½ cup (40g) shredded coconut, toasted
- ½ cup (110g) firmly packed brown sugar

LEMON CURD

- ⅓ cup (80ml) lemon juice
- 1 tablespoon cornflour (cornstarch)
- 270ml can coconut cream
- ¼ cup (60ml) pure maple syrup
- 2 pinches ground turmeric

1 Place green tea jasmine tea bags in a heatproof jug with 1⅔ cups (410ml) boiling water. Steep for 30 minutes or until water is lukewarm. Remove tea bags; discard. Stir lemon rind and 1 tablespoon of maple syrup into tea.

2 Combine flour, yeast, salt and cardamom in a large bowl. Make a well in the centre. Pour tea mixture into well; mix to a sticky dough. Transfer dough to a large oiled bowl; cover with plastic wrap. Refrigerate for 12 hours or overnight.

3 Make nut filling.

4 Turn dough out onto a well-floured surface; press out to a 24cm x 40cm (9½in x 16in) rectangle. Scatter with nut filling. Starting from one long end, roll dough up tightly to enclose filling. Cut log into 12 equal pieces. Place each piece, cut-side up, 1.5cm (¾in) apart (mixture will spread) in a greased 25cm (10in) springform cake pan. Cover loosely with oiled plastic wrap. Stand in a warm place for 1 hour or until dough has increased in size by one third.

5 Meanwhile, make lemon curd.

6 Preheat oven to 200°C/400°F.

7 Bake scrolls for 25 minutes. Brush tops with remaining maple syrup; bake for a further 5 minutes or until shiny and glossy.

8 Drizzle scrolls with 2 tablespoons lemon curd; top with extra grated lemon rind and chopped pistachios. Serve with remaining lemon curd.

nut filling Combine ingredients in a small bowl.

lemon curd Whisk lemon juice and cornflour in a small saucepan until over medium heat until smooth. Whisk in coconut cream, maple syrup and turmeric until combined; cook, whisking continuously, until mixture boils and thickens slightly. Reduce heat slightly; continue whisking for a further 5 minutes or until mixture is thick enough to coat the back of a spoon. Transfer to a bowl; cover surface directly with plastic wrap. Refrigerate until needed.

PREP + COOK TIME 55 MINUTES (+ OVERNIGHT STANDING) **SERVES** 4

TURMERIC DOSA WITH MASALA CAULIFLOWER

Dosa are pancakes made from a fermented mixture of rice and pulses. Masala is an Indian spice mix.

- 1 cup (195g) white long-grain rice
- ⅓ cup (65g) black lentils (urad dhal)
- 2 tablespoons yellow split peas
- 2 teaspoons sea salt flakes
- ½ teaspoon caster (superfine) sugar
- 1 teaspoon ground cumin
- ½ teaspoon ground turmeric
- ⅓ cup (80ml) olive oil

MINT CHUTNEY

- 4 cups fresh mint leaves
- 2 cloves garlic
- 2 teaspoons grated fresh ginger
- 3 fresh dates (60g), pitted
- 1 fresh long green chilli, chopped coarsely
- ⅓ cup (80ml) fresh lime juice
- ¼ cup (60ml) extra virgin olive oil

MASALA CAULIFLOWER

- 1 medium cauliflower (1.5kg), cut into small florets
- ⅓ cup (80ml) olive oil
- 1 medium red onion (170g), sliced thinly
- 1 teaspoon yellow mustard seeds
- 1 teaspoon ground turmeric
- ⅓ cup fresh curry leaves
- 1 fresh long green chilli, sliced thinly
- 1 tablespoon grated fresh ginger

1 To start making dosas, rinse rice, lentils and split peas in a sieve under cold running water until water runs clear; place in a large bowl. Cover generously with water; stand, covered, at room temperature overnight.

2 Strain rice mixture through a fine sieve. Place drained rice mixture in a food processor with 1¼ cups (310ml) water; process until it forms a slightly thick, grainy batter. Transfer to a large bowl. Stand, covered, at room temperature for 4 hours to ferment.

3 Start making mint chutney and masala cauliflower 30 minutes before serving.

4 Stir salt, sugar and spices into dosa batter.

5 Heat a 15cm (6in) non-stick frying pan over medium-high heat. Brush pan lightly with olive oil. Pour ⅓ cup batter into centre of pan. Immediately, and in a circular motion, spread batter from centre towards the edge of the pan, creating a thin pancake. Drizzle 1 teaspoon oil around the edges and on surface of dosa; cook for 3 minutes or until golden and crisp. Slide a spatula around edges of dosa and fold in half; slide on to a plate. Repeat with remaining batter and oil to make 12 dosas in total.

6 Fill dosas with masala cauliflower; serve with mint chutney.

mint chutney Process ingredients to a pesto-like consistency.

masala cauliflower Blanch cauliflower in a large saucepan of boiling water for 3 minutes or until just tender. Drain very well. Heat oil in a large frying pan over medium high heat; cook onion, stirring, for 5 minutes or until soft. Add mustard seeds; cook, stirring, for 1 minute or until seeds start to pop. Add turmeric, curry leaves, green chilli and ginger; cook, stirring, for 1 minute or until fragrant. Add 2 tablespoons water; stir until combined. Add drained cauliflower, stir until heated through.

tips If the dosa mixture is too thick add a little extra water. Instead of making your own dosas, use store-bought vegan flat bread instead.

serving ideas Serve with lime wedges, extra green chilli and curry leaves fried in a little hot oil for 10 seconds until crisp.

PALLARES
SOLSONA

PREP + COOK TIME 1 HOUR 30 MINUTES **SERVES** 8

LENTIL LOAF WITH MAPLE GLAZE

Serve the loaf as part of a ploughman's platter with pickled vegetables, beetroot dip and cornichons.

- **1 cup (200g) dried green lentils, rinsed**
- **½ cup (100g) brown rice**
- **3 cups (750ml) vegetable stock**
- **1 cup (100g) walnuts**
- **1 tablespoon extra virgin olive oil**
- **1 small red onion (100g), diced finely**
- **2 trimmed celery stalks (200g), diced finely**
- **1 clove garlic, crushed**
- **1 small apple (130g), grated finely**
- **¼ cup (40g) flaxseed meal**
- **¾ cup (90g) quick oats**
- **⅓ cup fresh thyme leaves**
- **⅓ cup (95g) tomato sauce (ketchup)**
- **2 tablespoons pure maple syrup**
- **2 tablespoons balsamic vinegar**

1 Preheat oven to 200°C/400°F. Oil a 12cm x 25cm (4¾in x 10in) loaf pan; line with baking paper.

2 Place lentils, rice and stock in a medium saucepan; bring to the boil. Reduce heat to medium; simmer gently for 40 minutes or until lentils and rice are tender and stock is absorbed.

3 Meanwhile, place walnuts on an oven tray; roast for 4 minutes or until golden. Cool; coarsely chop. Reduce oven to 160°C/325°F.

4 Heat olive oil in a medium frying pan; cook onion and celery, stirring, for 3 minutes or until soft. Add garlic and apple; cook for 5 minutes. Remove from heat.

5 Transfer lentil mixture to a large bowl with walnuts and onion mixture.

6 Combine flaxseed meal with ½ cup water in a small bowl until it becomes a gel-like consistency. Add to lentil mixture with oats and thyme, season with salt and peppe; stir well to combine. Spoon mixture into lined pan; smooth the surface.

7 Whisk tomato sauce, maple syrup and balsamic vinegar in a small bowl. Brush half the glaze mixture over the loaf. Cover with foil.

8 Bake loaf for 40 minutes. Remove the foil; brush with remaining glaze. Bake for a further 20 minutes or until top is browned. Transfer pan to a wire rack and allow to cool completely before slicing. Serve topped with extra thyme sprigs, if you like.

serving idea A great alternative to meatloaf, serve this load with mashed potato, steamed vegetables and a vegan gravy; any leftovers can be used as a sandwich filling with lettuce and tomato.

PREP + COOK TIME 1 HOUR 30 MINUTES SERVES 6

POMEGRANATE EGGPLANT WITH JEWELLED RICE

Pomegranates are in season in Autum, if unavailable, use halved small red grapes instead.

- ½ cup (100g) yellow dried split peas
- ¼ cup (60ml) extra virgin olive oil
- 2 medium onions (300g), sliced thinly
- 1 teaspoon sea salt flakes
- 650g (1¼lb) finger eggplants
- 4 ripe medium tomatoes (600g), chopped coarsely
- ¼ cup (75g) pomegranate molasses
- 3 cloves garlic, crushed
- 1 teaspoon ground turmeric
- 1 stick cinnamon
- 3 cups (750ml) vegetable stock
- ¼ cup fresh baby mint leaves
- ¼ cup fresh baby coriander (cilantro) leaves
- **JEWELLED RICE**
- 2 cups (400g) basmati rice
- 1 pinch saffron threads
- 1 tablespoon coconut oil
- 2 tablespoons pomegranate seeds
- 2 tablespoons pistachios, chopped coarsely

1 Preheat oven to 220°C/450°F. Line an oven tray with baking paper.

2 Place split peas in a large saucepan with 2 litres (8 cups) water; bring to boil. Reduce heat to low; simmer, covered, for 30 minutes or until tender but still holding their shape. Drain well.

3 Meanwhile, heat 2 tablespoons of the oil in a large, heavy-based saucepan over low-medium heat. Cook onions with a pinch of the salt for 20 minutes, stirring often to prevent sticking, or until soft and dark brown.

4 Meanwhile, cut eggplant in half lengthways; place on lined tray. Drizzle with remaining oil, sprinkle with remaining salt; toss on tray. Turn eggplant, cut-side down. Roast for 25 minutes or until flesh is very soft.

5 Add drained split peas and roasted eggplant to onion in pan with tomato, pomegranate molasses, garlic, turmeric and cinnamon. Stir in the stock; bring to a simmer. Reduce heat to low; cook for 40 minutes, stirring occasionally, or until thick.

6 Make jeweled rice.

7 Serve eggplant mixture on jewelled rice, topped with herbs.

jewelled rice Place rice in a fine sieve; rinse under cold running water until water runs clear. Place rice in a large saucepan with 3 cups (750ml) water, the saffron and a pinch of salt; bring to boil. Reduce heat to low; cook, covered, for 15 minutes or until water is absorbed. Remove from heat; stand, covered, for 10 minutes. Drizzle rice with coconut oil and fluff grains with a fork. Sprinkle with pomegranate seeds and pistachios.

PREP + COOK TIME 1 HOUR 10 MINUTES **SERVES** 4

UPSIDE DOWN RATATOUILLE TART

This tart is at its best eaten soon after baking, when the pastry is still crisp and warm.

- **¼ cup (60ml) extra virgin olive oil, plus extra to drizzle**
- **3 medium onions (450g), sliced thinly**
- **2 cloves garlic, sliced**
- **1 fresh long red chilli, sliced**
- **2 teaspoons fresh thyme leaves**
- **4 small roma (egg) tomatoes (240g), halved lengthways**
- **1 large zucchini (150g), cut into 1.5cm (¾in) rounds**
- **1 medium eggplant (300g), cut into 1.5cm (¾in) rounds**
- **1 tablespoon balsamic vinegar**
- **1½ sheets frozen puff pastry**
- **½ cup firmly packed fresh basil leaves**

1 Heat 2 tablespoons of the oil in a medium saucepan over medium heat. Add onion, garlic, chilli and thyme. Reduce heat to low; cook, stirring occasionally, for 30 minutes or until onions are soft and caramelised.

2 Preheat oven to 200°C/400°F. Line an oven tray with baking paper.

3 Place tomatoes, zucchini and eggplant on lined tray, drizzle with vinegar and remaining oil; season. Bake for 20 minutes or until vegetables are browned; remove from oven. Increase oven to 220°C/425°F.

4 Line a 20cm x 30cm (8in x 12in) slice pan with baking paper, extending the paper 2cm (¾in) over sides. Thaw pastry then join sheets together to form a long rectangle.

5 Place tomatoes, cut-side down, on base of lined pan with zucchini and eggplant to fit snuggly, side by side. Top with caramelised onion and half the basil leaves.

6 Place pastry over the vegetables and trim if necessary, leaving enough to tuck in around the inside edges of the pan.

7 Bake tart for 25 minutes or until pastry is puffed and golden. Leave in the pan for 5 minutes.

8 Place a board or platter large enough to cover the pan over the tart; flip tart onto board, then remove the lining paper. Drizzle tart with extra olive oil and top with remaining basil. Cut tart into four wedges to serve.

serving idea Top with vegan fetta and serve with a side salad.

Dip platters

SUPER GUACAMOLE

PREP TIME 10 MINUTES **MAKES** 2 CUPS

Place 1 fresh small finely chopped red chilli in a medium bowl with 1 small clove crushed garlic, ½ teaspoon ground cumin and 1 tablespoon lime juice. Add 2 medium (500g) avocados and ¼ cup finely chopped fresh coriander (cilantro); mash with a fork until combined. Transfer dip to a serving bowl; top with 1 teaspoon chia seeds, 2 tablespoons roasted pepitas (pumpkin seed kernels) and a few extra coriander leaves.

serving ideas Arrange dip on a platter with blue corn tortillas chips and baby radishes.

BEETROOT & WALNUT DIP

PREP + COOK TIME 1¼ HOURS **MAKES** 1¾ CUP

Preheat oven to 200°C/400°F. Scrub 2 medium (350g) beetroot (beets); wrap individually in foil. Place on an oven tray; roast for 40 minutes. Add 2 unpeeled cloves garlic to tray; roast for a further 20 minutes or until beetroot and garlic are tender. Stand beetroot until cool enough to handle. Peel beetroot; chop coarsely. Squeeze flesh from garlic. Process beetroot and garlic with 1 cup roasted walnuts, 2 tablespoons lemon juice and 1 tablespoon hulled tahini until smooth. Transfer dip to a bowl; top with extra walnuts.

serving ideas Arrange dip on a platter with cauliflower florets, baby (dutch) carrots and red witlof leaves.

Having one or two dips on a platter with an assortment of fresh cut up vegetables and crackers is an easy way to create an impressive spread with minimum effort.

CARROT & TURMERIC HUMMUS

PREP TIME 10 MINUTES **MAKES** 2 CUPS

Coarsely grate 1 medium (120g) carrot. Drain a 400g (12½oz) can chickpeas (garbanzo beans), then rinse well. Place carrot and chickpeas in a food processor with 1 tablespoon hulled tahini, 2 tablespoons lemon juice, 2 teaspoons grated fresh turmeric (or ½ teaspoon ground), ½ teaspoon ground cumin, 1 clove crushed garlic and ¼ cup extra virgin olive oil; process until smooth. Transfer dip to a bowl.

serving ideas Arrange dip on a platter with pitta bread, fennel wedges and baby cucumbers, halved lengthways.

MISO PEANUT BUTTER DIP

PREP TIME 5 MINUTES **MAKES** 1 CUP

Combine 2 tablespoons white (shiro) miso paste, ½ cup (140g) natural crunchy peanut butter, 2 tablespoons sesame oil, 1½ tablespoons rice wine vinegar and ¼ cup warm water in a medium bowl. Transfer dip to a bowl; sprinkle with sesame seeds. Serve immediately. If not serving immediately thin with a little extra warm water.

serving ideas Arrange dip on a platter with young celery stalks, blanched green beans and sugar snap peas.

PREP + COOK TIME 1 HOUR (+ STANDING) SERVES 10

VEGAN CHOCOLATE LAYER CAKE

This is an impressive and delicious cake that just happens to have no dairy or egg products in it.

- 2½ cups (375g) plain (all-purpose) flour
- 1 cup (125g) dutch-processed cocoa, plus extra for dusting
- 2 teaspoons baking powder
- ½ teaspoon bicarbonate of soda (baking soda)
- 2½ cups (375g) coconut sugar
- ⅔ cup (160ml) grapeseed oil
- 2⅔ cups (660ml) soy milk
- 2 tablespoons apple cider vinegar
- 1 tablespoon vanilla extract

CHOCOLATE FROSTING

- 1½ cup (300g) vegan butter-style margarine
- 2¼ cups (360g) icing (confectioners') sugar mixture
- ½ cup (50g) dutch-processed cocoa
- 1½ tablespoons soy milk
- 1½ teaspoons vanilla extract
- 1 pinch sea salt flakes

1 Preheat oven to 180°C/350°F. Grease two 20cm (8in) cake pans; line bases and sides with baking paper.

2 Combine sifted flour, cocoa, baking powder, bicarbonate of soda and coconut sugar in a large bowl. Whisk grapeseed oil, soy milk, vinegar and vanilla in a medium bowl. Add to dry ingredients; mix until just combined. Divide mixture between pans.

3 Bake cakes for 45 minutes or until a skewer inserted into the centre comes out clean. Leave in pans for 15 minutes before turning, top-side up, onto wire racks to cool.

4 Make chocolate frosting.

5 Place one cake on a cake plate; spread with half the frosting. Top with remaining cake; spread with remaining frosting. Just before serving, dust with extra cocoa.

chocolate frosting Beat ingredients in a medium bowl with an electric mixer until pale and creamy.

tip The un-iced cakes can be made a day ahead. Once cool, cover tightly with plastic wrap and store at room temperature.

serving ideas Decorate cake with squares of vegan chocolate and edible pink flowers.

PREP + COOK TIME 1 HOUR (+ REFRIGERATION) **SERVES** 4

WHITE BEAN & BEET GNOCCHI WITH RAINBOW CHARD RAGU

Chard and silver beet are identical in taste and similarly high in vitamins A, K, C and E

- **2 x 400g (12½oz) cans cannellini beans, drained, rinsed**
- **2 small cooked beetroot (400g) (see tip)**
- **¼ cup (60ml) extra virgin olive oil**
- **1½ teaspoons sea salt flakes**
- **1⅓ cup (150g) plain (all-purpose) flour, plus extra to dust**
- **20g (¾oz) dried porcini mushrooms, chopped**
- **1 bunch rainbow chard (750g)**
- **2 tablespoons extra virgin olive oil, extra**
- **1 medium leek (350g), sliced thinly**
- **2 cloves garlic, crushed**
- **1 tablespoon fresh thyme leaves, chopped**
- **2 tablespoons vegan parmesan (see page 17)**

1 To make gnocchi, process beans and beetroot to a coarse paste. Add olive oil and salt; pulse briefly until combined. Add flour; pulse briefly until mixture forms a dough. Transfer to a piece of plastic wrap; wrap to enclose. Refrigerate for 15 minutes.

2 Meanwhile, place porcini mushrooms in a small heatproof bowl with 1 cup (250ml) boiling water; soak for 15 minutes.

3 Remove stalks from chard; slice thinly, then finely shred leaves. Heat the extra olive oil in a large deep frying pan over medium heat; cook leek and chard stalks for 5 minutes or until softened. Add garlic and thyme; cook, stirring, for 1 minute. Add chard leaves, stir for 2 minutes. Add porcini and soaking liquid; simmer for 3 minutes or until liquid reduces. Season to taste; cover and keep warm.

4 Bring a large saucepan of salted water to the boil. On a lightly floured surface, divide gnocchi dough into four portions. Roll each portion into a 45cm (18in) log, then cut into 3cm (1¼in) pieces. Cook gnocchi, in two batches, for 4 minutes or until they rise to the surface. Remove with a slotted spoon.

5 Add cooked gnocchi to the chard ragu; stir gently to combine. Serve gnocchi and ragu, topped with vegan parmesan.

tip Ready cooked beetroot are sold in vacuum-sealed packs in the fresh food section in major supermarkets and specialist greengrocers.

food swap You can use silver beet (chard) instead of the rainbow chard.

serving idea Top gnocchi with micro herbs such as red sorrel.

PREP + COOK TIME 1 HOUR 25 MINUTES **SERVES** 4

ROASTED ROOT VEGIES WITH CARROT TOP COUSCOUS

Root vegies are available year round, but cool season crops are the best, especially for parsnips.

- 1 bunch multi coloured baby (dutch) carrots (350g), with tops attached
- 1 bunch baby beetroot (beets) (400g)
- 4 small parsnips (500g)
- 1 medium celeriac (celery root) (750g)
- 1 medium bulb garlic, halved horizontally
- 2 small sprig fresh rosemary
- ½ cup (125ml) extra virgin olive oil
- ¼ cup (60ml) pure maple syrup

CARROT TOP COUSCOUS

- 1 tablespoon extra virgin olive oil
- 1 cup (200g) pearl couscous
- 2 cups (500ml) vegetable stock
- 1 cup reserved chopped carrot tops (from step 2)
- ⅓ cup (45g) pistachios

1 Preheat oven to 180°C/350°F.

2 Trim tops from carrots; wash and dry well with paper towel. Coarsely chop tops; you will need 1 cup. Reserve for carrot top couscous.

3 Peel baby carrots, beetroot and parsnips. Cut any large carrots in half lengthways. Halve or quarter beetroot if large. Halve parsnips lengthways. Cut celeriac into 4cm (1½in) chunks. Divide vegetables between two roasting pans. Add garlic halves and rosemary; drizzle with oil, season. Cover pans with foil.

4 Roast vegetables for 40 minutes. Remove foil, drizzle with maple syrup; roast for a further 20 minutes or until tender and golden.

5 Meanwhile, make couscous.

6 Serve vegetables drizzled with the pan juices and carrot top couscous.

carrot top couscous Heat oil in a medium saucepan over medium heat; cook couscous, stirring, for 2 minutes. Add stock; bring to the boil. Cook, covered, over low heat for 10 minutes or until liquid is absorbed. Season to taste. Add reserved carrot tops and the pistachios; stir to combine.

serving ideas Top vegetables with kale leaves, baby spinach leaves or flat-leaf parsley.

PREP + COOK TIME 3 HOURS (+ OVERNIGHT STANDING) **SERVES** 4

SLOW-COOKED MAPLE BOSTON BEANS WITH SOFT POLENTA

To keep polenta warm, pour into a stainless steel bowl; cover with foil, place on a pan of simmering water.

- 375g (12oz) dried white beans
- ¼ cup (60ml) olive oil
- 2 large onions (400g), chopped finely
- 4 cloves garlic, crushed
- 2 fresh bay leaves
- 2 tablespoons smoked paprika
- 1 tablespoon ground cumin
- 2 tablespoons dijon mustard
- 2 tablespoons apple cider vinegar
- ¼ cup (60ml) pure maple syrup
- 400g (12½oz) can diced tomatoes
- 1 litre (4 cups) vegetable stock
- 2 tablespoons vegan worcestershire sauce (see vegan hacks)
- ⅓ cup (80ml) smokey barbecue sauce

SOFT POLENTA

- 3 cups (750ml) vegetable stock
- 3 cups (750ml) almond milk
- 1 cup (170g) polenta (cornmeal)
- 1 teaspoon sea salt flakes

1 Place dried beans in a large bowl with enough water to cover. Stand for 8 hours or overnight. Drain.

2 Heat olive oil a large saucepan over medium heat; cook onion for 8 minutes or until soft and golden. Add garlic and bay leaves; cook for 2 minutes or until fragrant.

3 Stir paprika and ground cumin into onion mixture, then drained beans and remaining ingredients; bring to the boil. Reduce heat to low; cook, covered, for 2½ hours, stirring occasionally, or until beans are tender and sauce is thick.

4 Make soft polenta.

5 Serve beans with polenta.

soft polenta Place stock and almond milk in a large saucepan; bring to the boil. Gradually stir in polenta. Reduce heat to low; cook, stirring frequently, for 20 minutes or until soft and smooth. Stir in salt; season with pepper.

vegan hacks If you don't have enough time to soak the beans for 8 hours in step 1, place the beans in a saucepan with enough water to cover them by 5cm (2in); bring to the boil, then boil for 15 minutes. Remove from heat and stand until cooled. Continue as instructed in the recipe. Vegan worcestershire sauce is available from some major supermarkets and online; check the brand label carefully to ensure it does not contain anchovies. If unavailable, use tamari instead.

serving ideas Top with baby spinach leaves and fresh thyme or chopped flat-leaf parsley.

Glossary

AGAVE SYRUP from the agave plant; has a low GI, but that is due to the high percentage of fructose present, which may be harmful in large quantities.

ALMONDS

blanched brown skins removed.

flaked paper-thin slices.

meal nuts are powdered to a coarse flour-like texture.

slivered small pieces cut lengthways.

ARROWROOT a starch made from the rhizome of a Central American plant, used mostly as a thickening agent.

BAKING POWDER a raising agent consisting mainly of two parts cream of tartar to one part bicarbonate of soda.

BARLEY a nutritious grain used in soups and stews. Hulled barley, the least processed, is high in fibre. Pearl barley has had the husk removed then been steamed and polished so that only the 'pearl' of the original grain remains, much the same as white rice.

BEANS

black also called turtle beans or black kidney beans; an earthy-flavoured dried bean completely different from the better-known Chinese black beans (fermented soybeans). Used mostly in Mexican and South American cooking.

borlotti also called roman beans or pink beans, can be eaten fresh or dried. Interchangeable with pinto beans due to their similarity in appearance – pale pink or beige with dark red streaks.

cannellini small white bean similar in appearance and flavour to other phaseolus vulgaris varieties (great northern, navy or haricot). Available dried or canned.

soy the most nutritious of all legumes; high in protein and low in carbohydrate and the source of products such as tofu, soy milk, soy sauce, tamari and miso. Sometimes sold fresh as edamame; also available dried and canned. *see also* edamame

sprouts tender new growths of assorted beans and seeds germinated for consumption as sprouts.

BICARBONATE OF SODA (baking soda) a raising agent.

BUCKWHEAT a herb in the same plant family as rhubarb; not a cereal so it is gluten-free. Available as flour; ground (cracked) into coarse, medium or fine granules (kasha) and used similarly to polenta; or groats, the whole kernel sold roasted as a cereal product.

CACAO

butter is rich in saturated fats; about a third is stearic acid, but this acts differently to other saturated fats in that it doesn't raise cholesterol and, in fact, lowers LDL (bad) cholesterol. It is available from some health food stores and gourmet food stores.

nibs can be separated into cocoa butter and powder. Cocoa powder retains many beneficial antioxidants and is an easy way of adding cocoa into your diet without the kilojoules of chocolate.

powder is made by removing the cocoa butter using a process known as cold-pressing. It retains more of its nutrients than heat-processed cacao powder; it also has a stronger, slightly bitter, taste.

CASHEWS plump, kidney-shaped, golden-brown nuts having a distinctive sweet, buttery flavour and containing about 48% fat. Because of this high fat content, they should be kept, sealed tightly, under refrigeration to avoid becoming rancid. Roasting cashews brings out their intense nutty flavour.

CHIA SEEDS contain protein and all the essential amino acids and a wealth of vitamins, minerals and antioxidants, as well as being fibre-rich.

CHICKPEAS (GARBANZO BEANS) also called hummus or channa; an irregularly round, sandy-coloured legume used extensively in Mediterranean, Indian and Hispanic cooking. Firm texture even after cooking, a floury mouth-feel and robust nutty flavour; available canned or dried (reconstitute for several hours in cold water before use).

CHILLI available in many different types and sizes. Use rubber gloves when seeding and chopping fresh chillies as they can burn your skin. Removing seeds and membranes lessens the heat level.

chipotle pronounced cheh-pote-lay. The name used for jalapeño chillies once they've been dried and smoked. Having a deep, intensely smokey flavour, rather than a searing heat, chipotles are dark brown, almost black in colour and wrinkled in appearance.

green any unripened chilli; also some particular varieties that are ripe when green, such as jalapeño, habanero, poblano or serrano.

jalapeño pronounced hah-lah-pain-yo. Fairly hot, medium-sized, plump, dark green chilli; available pickled, sold canned or bottled, and fresh, from greengrocers.

long red available both fresh and dried; a generic term used for any moderately hot, long, thin chilli (about 6cm to 8cm long).

COCONUT

cream comes from the first pressing of the coconut flesh, without the addition of water; the second pressing (less rich) is sold as coconut milk. Look for coconut cream labelled as 100% coconut, without added emulsifiers.

desiccated concentrated, dried, unsweetened and finely shredded coconut flesh.

flaked dried flaked coconut flesh.

milk not the liquid found inside the fruit (coconut water), but the diluted liquid from the second pressing of the white flesh of a mature coconut (the first pressing produces coconut cream).

oil is extracted from the coconut flesh so you don't get any of the fibre, protein or carbohydrates present in the whole coconut. The best quality is virgin coconut oil, which is the oil pressed from the dried coconut flesh, and doesn't include the use of solvents or other refining processes.

shredded thin strips of dried coconut.
sugar *see* Sugar
water is the liquid from the centre of a young green coconut. It has fewer kilojoules than fruit juice, with no fat or protein. There are sugars present, but these are slowly absorbed giving coconut water a low GI.

CORNFLOUR (CORNSTARCH) available made from corn or wheat (wheaten cornflour, which contains gluten, gives a lighter texture in cakes); used as a thickening agent in cooking.

CUMIN also known as zeera or comino; resembling a caraway in size, cumin is the dried seed of a plant related to the parsley family and has a spicy, nutty flavour. Available as seeds, dried and ground.

EDAMAME (shelled soy beans) available frozen from Asian food stores and some supermarkets.

EGGPLANT also called aubergine. Ranging in size from tiny to very large and in colour from pale green to deep purple.

FENNEL a roundish, bulbous vegetable, about 8-12cm in diameter, with a mild licorice smell and taste. The bulb has a slightly sweet, anise flavour but the leaves have a much stronger taste. Also the name given to dried seeds having a licorice flavour.

FLOUR
chickpea (besan) creamy yellow flour made from chickpeas and is very nutritious.
plain (all-purpose) a general all-purpose wheat flour.
rice very fine, almost powdery, gluten-free flour; made from ground white rice. Used in baking, as a thickener, and in some Asian noodles and desserts.
self-raising plain flour sifted with baking powder in the proportion of 1 cup flour to 2 teaspoons baking powder.
tapioca made from the root of the cassava plant; a soft, fine, light white flour.
wholemeal also known as wholewheat flour; milled with the wheat germ so is higher in fibre and more nutritional than plain flour.

FREEKEH is cracked roasted green wheat and can be found in some larger supermarkets, health food and specialty food stores.

GARAM MASALA a blend of spices that includes cardamom, cloves, cumin, cinnamon, coriander, and fennel. Black pepper and chilli can also be added for heat.

GAI LAN also called gai larn, chinese broccoli and chinese kale; green vegetable appreciated more for its stems than its coarse leaves. Can be served steamed and stir-fried, in soups and noodle dishes.

GINGER
fresh also called green or root ginger; the thick gnarled root of a tropical plant. Can be kept, peeled, covered with dry sherry in a jar and refrigerated, or frozen in an airtight container.
ground also called powdered ginger; used as a flavouring in baking but cannot be substituted for fresh ginger.
pickled pink or red coloured; available, packaged, from Asian food shops. Pickled paper-thin shavings of ginger in a mixture of vinegar, sugar and natural colouring; used in Japanese cooking.

HARISSA a Moroccan paste made from dried chillies, cumin, garlic, oil and caraway seeds. Available from Middle Eastern food shops and supermarkets.

HAZELNUTS also known as filberts; plump, grape-sized, rich, sweet nut having a brown skin that is removed by rubbing heated nuts together vigorously in a tea-towel.
meal is made by grounding the hazelnuts to a coarse flour texture for use in baking or as a thickening agent.

LENTILS (red, brown, yellow) dried pulses often identified by and named after their colour. Eaten by cultures all over the world, most famously perhaps in the dhals of India.
French-style a local cousin to the famous (and very expensive) French lentils du puy; green-blue, tiny lentils with a nutty, earthy flavour and a hardy nature that allows them to be rapidly cooked without disintegrating.

LINSEEDS also known as flaxseeds, they are the richest plant source of omega 3 fats, which are essential for a healthy brain, heart, joints and immune system.

MACADAMIAS native to Australia; fairly large, slightly soft, buttery rich nut. Used to make oil and macadamia butter; equally good in salads or cakes and pastries; delicious eaten on their own.

MAPLE SYRUP also called pure maple syrup; distilled from the sap of sugar maple trees found only in Canada and the USA. Maple-flavoured syrup or pancake syrup is not an adequate substitute for the real thing.

MILLET is a small-seeded cereal grain, which has a slightly nutty, corn-like flavour. Puffed millet are grains that have been processed under high pressure with steam, causing them to expand and puff; it is available from health food stores and the health food section of large supermarkets.

MISO fermented soybean paste. There are many types of miso, each with its own aroma, flavour, colour and texture; it can be kept, airtight, for up to ayear in the fridge. Buy in tubs or plastic packs.

MUSHROOMS
button small, cultivated white mushrooms with a mild flavour.
enoki also known as enokitake, also enokidake; is a long, thin white mushroom used in East Asian cuisine.
oyster also known as abalone; grey-white mushrooms shaped like a fan. Prized for their smooth texture and subtle, oyster-like flavour.
portobello are mature, fully opened swiss browns; they are larger and bigger in flavour.

shiitake are also known as Chinese black, forest or golden oak mushrooms. Although cultivated, they have the earthiness and taste of wild mushrooms.
swiss brown also known as cremini or roman mushrooms; are light brown mushrooms with a full-bodied flavour.
NORI a type of dried seaweed used as a flavouring, garnish or for sushi. Sold in thin sheets, plain or toasted (yaki-nori).
NUTRITIONAL YEAST FLAKES a seasoning used to provide a moreish cheese-like umami taste. They are a complete protein and a good source of B vitamins. Look for a brand that is fortified with B12, a vitamin required for the development of healthy blood cells and the prevention of anaemia, which is only available from fortified foods or via a supplement on a vegan diet. Nutritional yeast flakes are available from health food stores.
OIL
coconut *see* Coconut
olive made from ripened olives. Extra virgin and virgin are the first and second press, respectively, of the olives; "light" refers to taste not fat levels.
peanut pressed from ground peanuts; most commonly used oil in Asian cooking because of its high smoke point (capacity to handle high heat without burning).
rice bran is extracted from the germ and inner husk of the rice grain; has a mild, slightly nutty, flavour. Its high smoke point means it's suitable for high-temperature cooking methods such as stir frying and deep frying.
sesame used as a flavouring rather than a cooking medium.
vegetable oils sourced from plant fats.
ONIONS
green (scallions) also called, incorrectly, shallot; an immature onion picked before the bulb has formed, has a long, bright-green stalk.
red also known as spanish, red spanish or bermuda onion; a sweet-flavoured, large, purple-red onion.
shallots also called french or golden shallots or eschalots; small and brown-skinned.
POLENTA also known as cornmeal; a flour-like cereal made of ground corn (maize). Also the name of the dish made from it.
QUINOA is the seed of a leafy plant similar to spinach. It has a delicate, slightly nutty taste and chewy texture.
RICE MALT SYRUP also known as brown rice syrup or rice syrup; is made by cooking brown rice flour with enzymes to break down its starch into sugars from which the water is removed.
ROASTING/TOASTING desiccated coconut, pine nuts and sesame seeds roast more evenly if stirred over low heat in a heavy-based frying pan; their natural oils will help turn them golden brown. Remove from pan immediately. Nuts and dried coconut can be roasted in the oven to release their aromatic essential oils. Spread evenly onto an oven tray; roast at 180°C/350°F for about 5 minutes.
SESAME SEEDS black and white are the most common of this small oval seed, however there are also red and brown varieties. The seeds are used as an ingredient and as a condiment. Toast the seeds in a heavy-based frying pan over low heat.
SUGAR
brown very soft, finely granulated sugar retaining molasses for its characteristic colour and flavour.
caster (superfine) finely granulated table sugar.
coconut is not made from coconuts, but from the sap of the blossoms of the coconut palm tree. The refined sap looks a little like raw or light brown sugar, and has a similar caramel flavour. It also has the same amount of kilojoules as regular table (white) sugar.
icing (confectioners') also called powdered sugar; pulverised white sugar crushed with a small amount of cornflour (cornstarch).
palm also called nam tan pip, jaggery, jawa or gula melaka; made from the sap of the sugar palm tree. Light brown to black in colour and usually sold in rock-hard cakes; use brown sugar if unavailable.
TAHINI a rich, sesame-seed paste, used in most Middle-Eastern cuisines, especially Lebanese, in dips and sauces.
TAMARI a thick, dark soy sauce made mainly from soya beans, but without the wheat used in most standard soy sauces.
TEMPEH a traditional soy product originating from Indonesia. It is made by a natural culturing and controlled fermentation process that binds soybeans into a cake form.
TOFU also called bean curd; an off-white, custard-like product made from the "milk" of crushed soybeans. Comes fresh as soft or firm, and processed as fried or pressed dried sheets. Fresh tofu can be refrigerated in water (changed daily) for up to 4 days.
firm made by compressing bean curd to remove most of the water. Good used in stir-fries as it can be tossed without disintegrating. Can also be flavoured, preserved in rice wine or brine.
silken not a type of tofu but reference to the manufacturing process of straining soybean liquid through silk; this denotes best quality.
TURMERIC also called kamin; is a rhizome related to galangal and ginger. Must be grated or pounded to release its acrid aroma and pungent flavour. Known for the golden colour it imparts, fresh turmeric can be substituted with the more commonly found dried powder. When fresh turmeric is called for in a recipe, the dried powder can be substituted (proportions are 1 teaspoon of ground turmeric for every 20g of fresh turmeric).
VANILLA
bean dried, long, thin pod from a tropical golden orchid; the minuscule black seeds inside the bean impart a luscious flavour.
extract obtained from vanilla beans infused in water; a non-alcoholic version of essence.
paste made from vanilla beans and contains real seeds. Is highly concentrated: 1 teaspoon replaces a whole vanilla bean. Found in most supermarkets in the baking section.
VINEGAR
apple cider made from fermented apples.
balsamic made from the juice of Trebbiano grapes; it is a deep rich brown colour with a sweet and sour flavour.
rice wine made from rice wine lees, salt and alcohol.
WASABI an Asian horseradish used to make the pungent, green-coloured sauce traditionally served with Japanese raw fish dishes; sold in powdered or paste form.
ZUCCHINI also called courgette.

Conversion chart

MEASURES

One Australian metric measuring cup holds approximately 250ml; one Australian metric tablespoon holds 20ml; one Australian metric teaspoon holds 5ml.

The difference between one country's measuring cups and another's is within a two- or three-teaspoon variance, and will not affect your cooking results. North America, New Zealand and the United Kingdom use a 15ml tablespoon.

All cup and spoon measurements are level. The most accurate way of measuring dry ingredients is to weigh them. When measuring liquids, use a clear glass or plastic jug with the metric markings.
We use large eggs with an average weight of 60g.

DRY MEASURES

metric	imperial
15g	½oz
30g	1oz
60g	2oz
90g	3oz
125g	4oz (¼lb)
155g	5oz
185g	6oz
220g	7oz
250g	8oz (½lb)
280g	9oz
315g	10oz
345g	11oz
375g	12oz (¾lb)
410g	13oz
440g	14oz
470g	15oz
500g	16oz (1lb)
750g	24oz (1½lb)
1kg	32oz (2lb)

LIQUID MEASURES

metric	imperial
30ml	1 fluid oz
60ml	2 fluid oz
100ml	3 fluid oz
125ml	4 fluid oz
150ml	5 fluid oz
190ml	6 fluid oz
250ml	8 fluid oz
300ml	10 fluid oz
500ml	16 fluid oz
600ml	20 fluid oz
1000ml (1 litre)	1¾ pints

LENGTH MEASURES

metric	imperial
3mm	⅛in
6mm	¼in
1cm	½in
2cm	¾in
2.5cm	1in
5cm	2in
6cm	2½in
8cm	3in
10cm	4in
13cm	5in
15cm	6in
18cm	7in
20cm	8in
22cm	9in
25cm	10in
28cm	11in
30cm	12in (1ft)

OVEN TEMPERATURES

The oven temperatures in this book are for conventional ovens; if you have a fan-forced oven, decrease the temperature by 10-20 degrees.

	°C (Celsius)	°F (Fahrenheit)
Very slow	120	250
Slow	150	300
Moderately slow	160	325
Moderate	180	350
Moderately hot	200	400
Hot	220	425
Very hot	240	475

Index

M

N

O

P

Q

R

S

T

U

V

W

Z

PUBLISHED IN 2018 BY BAUER MEDIA BOOKS, AUSTRALIA.
BAUER MEDIA BOOKS IS A DIVISION OF BAUER MEDIA PTY LTD.

Bauer Media Group

CHIEF EXECUTIVE OFFICER
PAUL DYKZEUL

CHIEF FINANCIAL OFFICER
ANDREW STEDWELL

Bauer Media Books

PUBLISHER
SALLY EAGLE

EDITORIAL & FOOD DIRECTOR
SOPHIA YOUNG

CREATIVE DIRECTOR & DESIGNER
HANNAH BLACKMORE

MANAGING EDITOR
STEPHANIE KISTNER

FOOD EDITOR
SOPHIA YOUNG

OPERATIONS MANAGER
DAVID SCOTTO

PHOTOGRAPHER
JEREMY SIMONS

STYLISTS
EMMA KNOWLES, SOPHIA YOUNG

PHOTOCHEFS
TESSA IMMENS, ANGELA DEVLIN

PHOTOCHEF ASSISTANT
NADIA FONOFF

RECIPE DEVELOPERS
JANE HOWARD, JORDANNA LEVIN, ANGELA DEVLIN, CARLY SOPHIA TAYLOR, WARREN MENDES, BREE HUTCHINS, TESSA IMMENS, ELIZABETH FIDUCIA, NADIA FONOFF, SARAH MURPHY

WITH THANKS
RL FOOTE DESIGN STUDIO, FOR THEIR BEAUTIFUL CERAMICS
WWW.RLFOOTEDESIGN.COM

PRINTED IN CHINA
BY LEO PAPER PRODUCTS LTD

A CATALOGUE RECORD FOR THIS BOOK IS AVAILABLE FROM THE NATIONAL LIBRARY OF AUSTRALIA.
ISBN 9781742459981 (PAPERBACK)

PUBLISHED BY BAUER MEDIA BOOKS,
A DIVISION OF BAUER MEDIA PTY LTD,
54 PARK ST, SYDNEY; GPO BOX 4088,
SYDNEY, NSW 2001, AUSTRALIA
PH +61 2 9282 8618; FAX +61 2 9126 3702
WWW.AWWCOOKBOOKS.COM.AU

INTERNATIONAL RIGHTS MANAGER
SIMONE AQUILINA
SAQUILINA@BAUER-MEDIA.COM.AU
PH +61 2 8268 6278

ORDER BOOKS
PHONE 136 116 (WITHIN AUSTRALIA)

OR ORDER ONLINE AT
WWW.AWWCOOKBOOKS.COM.AU

SEND RECIPE ENQUIRIES TO
RECIPEENQUIRIES@
BAUER-MEDIA.COM.AU

IN PARTNERSHIP WITH ANIMALS AUSTRALIA.

Animals Australia
for a *kinder* world

WWW.ANIMALSAUSTRALIA.ORG